Reader's Digest · National

Nature Notebooks

GARDEN AND WOODLAND BIRDS

Reader's Digest · National Trust

Nature Notebooks

GARDEN AND WOODLAND BIRDS

Published by The Reader's Digest Association Limited, London,
in association with The National Trust

GARDEN AND WOODLAND BIRDS
is a Reader's Digest Publication based upon The Reader's Digest
Nature Lover's Library Copyright © 1981 The Reader's Digest
Association Limited, London

First Edition
Copyright © 1986
The Reader's Digest Association Limited
25 Berkeley Square
London W1X 6AB

Additional editorial work by Duncan Petersen Publishing Limited,
5 Botts Mews, London W2 5AG.
Typesetting by Modern Reprographics Limited, Hull, North
Humberside.
Separations by Modern Reprographics Limited, (covers)
and Mullis Morgan Limited, London (duplicate film)
Printed by Everbest Printing Company Limited, Hong Kong

The illustration on the cover is of Killerton by Michael Woods.

CONTENTS

Using This Book   6-7

Identifying Birds: Basic Fieldcraft   8-10

The Birds   11-95

The Sites   96-120

Understanding birds and Recording Techniques   121-23

Glossary   124

Index   126

Acknowledgements   128

Using this book

By a happy coincidence, Britain is not only rich in gardens, parks and woodland, but The National Trust (and other conservation organizations featured in this book), own or manage many of the finest. Moreover, gardens and parks, including those of historic houses and castles, make excellent bird-watching, as does woodland. Together they are perhaps the most practical choice of habitats in which to start a lifetime's interest in birds.

This book enables you not only to identify, and to learn about garden and woodland birds, but lists sites where you may be able to see them. The field guide section, pages 12-95, works hand-in-hand with the sites gazetteer, pages 96-120, by means of the panel on each field guide page. The panel includes a brief general note on each species – often describing the bird's nest. A nest affords the naturalist an excellent opportunity for watching and identifying birds, but we would stress how essential it is not to approach too close to the nest.

Below the caption we list a sequence of numbers directing you to sites described in the gazetteer, in all of which you have an excellent chance of seeing the bird in question. They are not the *only* sites where you will see it, but they are the most interesting ones. Equally, you will find some species cross-referenced to a site, but not mentioned in the site description: space in the gazetteer tends to be restricted.

In certain cases, comparisons are made between the appearance or habits of a garden or woodland bird and those of a bird not included in this book. This is for the benefit of those who may possess the two other books in this series:

Seaside and Moorland Birds and *River, Wetland and Lowland Birds*

Those two titles also contain some woodland sites, and for this reason are well worth owning along with this book. However, their woodland habitats are rather more specialized in nature, the woodland being mainly associated with upland country, or with rivers and lakes.

The selection of species
The 84 birds chosen for the field guide section are by no means all the garden and woodland birds that can be seen in Britain; however, they are a representative selection of the most familiar of such species, and they are the most likely to be seen by the visitor without local knowledge. Among them are a fair sprinkling of uncommon birds, but also birds which, though rare on a nation-wide basis, can easily be seen if you visit the site which specializes in them. Where no specific sites are mentioned, the bird is either so common that it can be seen at the majority of sites, or so rare that its nesting areas are deliberately kept secret.

The selection of sites
The places described for bird-watching in the gazetteer section are, in England and Wales, primarily National Trust property. They have the excellent advantage of generally easy access, though it should also be realized that much of the land is not for the public to roam freely. Viewing is in many places from roads only, or from footpaths and tracks which are public rights of way. For this reason, a large scale map, such as the Ordnance Survey Landranger sheet (scale 1:50 000) is extremely useful since it shows footpaths which are public rights of way.

The Scottish sites are either Nature Reserves or Bird Sanctuaries to which the public generally has easy access – without membership of an organization or possessing a special permit. In addition to the National Trust sites in England and Wales, there are also featured a number of first-class properties owned or managed by other bodies: these are intended to make the coverage more comprehensive, both in terms of geographical spread and number of species covered.

The panel for notes
The space at the foot of each colour plate on pages 12-95 is a convenient introduction to the excellent – some would say essential – habit of making notes of bird observations. Individual headings are given for all the most important types of information needing to be logged when seeing a bird: location, time of day, weather, behaviour, and so on; but most important of all is the blank space left free for a sketch. However feeble you believe your artistic efforts may be, they are always worth making: a sketch forces you to recall, or to note specific aspects of a bird in detail.

The colour plates
The superb bird illustrations on pages 12-95 give you not only close-up, but also distant views of every species, and this is of course invaluable.

There are sometimes marked differences between the plumages of males and females of the same species, or between their winter and summer or adult and juvenile plumages.

Admission

Some of the sites featured in the gazetteer section are linked with an historic house or castle to which there is an admission charge. Full information on opening hours and admission fees is published in the following annual publications: *National Trust Properties Open* and The National Trust for Scotland's *Guide to Over One Hundred Properties.*

The distribution maps

The map on each colour plate shows you when and where you are most likely to see the species. The time of year when you see a bird, or the part of Britain where you see it, can be useful clues.

Red dots show breeding colonies.
Red shading shows the usual breeding range of summer visitors.
Green shows the usual breeding range of species present in Britain all year round.
Blue shows the areas where a species is found in winter.
Shading indicates where passage migrants occur – those species which stop in Britain while moving to or from breeding or wintering grounds outside Britain.

THE NATIONAL TRUST AND ITS WORK

The National Trust, a private charity founded in 1895, can claim to be the oldest conservation organization in the country. As well as caring for historic houses, castles and gardens, it owns 500,000 acres of land throughout England, Wales and Northern Ireland. With such extensive holdings it is not surprising that it owns many superb examples of each of the main habitat types in Britain: coasts, woods, uplands, heaths, grasslands, lakes, rivers and mires. It·acquired its first nature reserve, Wicken Fen, as early as 1895, and by 1910 had 13 properties of particular wildlife value. It now owns some 90 nature reserves, over 400 Sites of Special Scientific Interest (SSSIs) and many other properties of great interest, not only for birds, but for a great range of animal and plant communities.

The National Trust for Scotland, a separate organization, but with similar aims and objectives, was established in 1931 and owns 100,000 acres, including some of the finest mountain and coastal scenery in Scotland.

The Royal Society for the Protection of Birds (RSPB) and the Royal Society for Nature Conservation (RSNC) which, like the National Trusts, are charities with no direct government funding, have also been actively involved in wildlife conservation for many decades. The RSPB was founded in 1889 and manages over a hundred reserves covering 130,000 acres. The RSNC, established in 1912, acts as a national association for 46 Nature Conservation Trusts which between them manage over 1,600 nature reserves covering 1,120,000 acres.

Most of our woods require management if their unique value is to be maintained – their contribution to the landscape, their rich wildlife resource, and their value as places for the general public to enjoy. These three objectives – landscape, wildlife and access – are central to the management policies of The National Trust. Timber production, regarded by many as the traditional purpose of woodland management, is a lesser priority.

Woodland management for birds must revolve around two main features: structure, and species of tree. The greatest management need in many woods which have been neglected for years, or heavily grazed preventing natural regeneration, is to introduce young trees amongst the old, gradually and with the minimum amount of disturbance to the wildlife or landscape.

The policy of the National Trust to allow public access to its properties produces surprisingly few conflicts with wildlife conservation, although birds (along with particularly shy mammals, such as otter) are more prone to disturbance than other groups among our fauna and flora. Where important breeding or feeding sites are recognized, car park size can be deliberately restricted to limit the number of visitors, and footpaths re-routed.

Visits to the National Trust properties described in this book, together with those managed by other conservation organizations, should provide opportunities not only to appreciate the exceptionally rich and varied birdlife of British woodlands and gardens, but also to understand the care and resources which go into their management.

Katherine Hearn,
Assistant Adviser on Conservation,
The National Trust.

Identifying Birds: Basic Fieldcraft

To identify birds successfully, you need to concentrate your powers of observation on several distinct aspects of a given species. Probably the two most important are distinguishing, or diagnostic, field marks, and relative size. The pictures and captions on pages 9 and 10 will help you get to grips with these basic concepts. Of course, you will also need to be aware of, and observe, overall plumage colour, bill shape and size, flight pattern, song and behaviour. Building up a working knowledge of these is largely a matter of experience; and of capitalizing on that experience by taking notes – see page 6.

But clearly, if you are too far away from the bird to see or hear it, all the ornithological knowledge in the world is of little practical value. You need, in addition, some skill in fieldcraft – the art of being in the right place at the right time. Its object is to get you close enough to make a positive identification, either on the spot, or later with the help of notes and a field guide.

There is no great mystery in fieldcraft – most of it is simple commonsense, and many of the techniques described below will be familiar to anyone who has spent time watching birds feeding in a garden or local park.

Fieldcraft starts before you even leave home on a bird-watching trip: time spent in planning and preparation is never wasted. Check the weather report: forecasts of rain or poor visibility could mean disappointment. Plan your journey so that, if possible, you arrive at your destination early – song is a valuable clue, and is at its loudest early in the day.

This is also the time to sort out clothing and footwear suitable for the trip. Choose inconspicuous clothes in camouflage colours, rather than bright hues which attract attention. Try also to find clothing that doesn't rustle – some garments made from artificial fibre make a noise each time you move.

Take footwear that is suited to the terrain you are visiting: gum boots are ideal for wet woodlands, but create noise in dry leaves.

Though you can often identify a bird with the naked eye, binoculars make the process much easier. When choosing a pair, look for the two engraved numbers – such as 10 × 50. The smaller number indicates magnification; the larger number, the lens diameter, and thus the light-gathering power of the binoculars. For the novice bird-watcher, 8 × 30s are a sound choice. They are easy to focus, gather sufficient light even for use at dusk, and are not too heavy to carry round all day. Before buying a pair, though, it is wise to try other people's binoculars and see which you prefer.

Try to buy binoculars from a friendly, co-operative dealer, and ask him to let you compare the sharpness of different makes by focusing on, say, a sheet of newspaper pinned up 20 yards (18 m) away. Also compare brightness of image, weight, general handling and whether suited to the wearer of spectacles.

In the field

Once you are on the spot, try to identify the most promising area to watch from. Of course, if you are simply observing birds in your own garden, or in a small local park, the choice is made for you. But in a large area of mixed woodland, for example, the decision may be more difficult because there are more options from which to choose.

There are a few general rules that you will find helpful: probably the most important is to find a spot from which you can observe the greatest possible variety of habitats. Clearings or broad rides through the trees are usually more rewarding than dense woodlands, not just because of the sheer difficulty of looking through thick foliage, but because open areas support a greater range of species.

Look down at the ground for another clue to an area's population. The more dead branches and leaves there are, the more birds you are likely to see, since many species feed on the insects that breed in rotting vegetation and wood. Brambles and shrubs at ground level are valuable, too – they provide protection, nesting sites and food.

The actual mix of tree and shrub species is important, and as a general rule, the more variety there is the better. Single species Forestry-Commission conifer plantations, for example, have very little birdlife to speak of. The other end of the spectrum is ancient mixed woodland supporting numerous different kinds of tree, shrub, plant and fungus. In these areas it is possible to see an exciting range of birds. Out of the woods, look for old hedgerows – these, too, support many birds.

Having found a good place from which to watch, keep absolutely still for some minutes. Before long, your presence will seem less threatening to birds in the area, and you will begin to see more signs of activity. In spring and summer, foliage will almost certainly hide much of the bird population from

Knowing what to look for is the key to success in identifying birds. The size, shape and colouring of a bird are the first and most obvious clues to its identity. But how it stands or moves, how it swims or flies, how it sings, feeds or approaches its mate – these and other aspects of its behaviour may be just as distinctive as its plumage. The time of year, and the place where the bird is seen, are also identification points. Some birds only visit Britain at particular times of the year, coming from breeding or wintering grounds that may be thousands of miles away. Other birds are so well adapted to life in a particular habitat that they are only rarely encountered outside it.

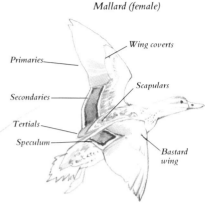

Mallard (female)

Primaries

Wing coverts

Secondaries

Scapulars

Tertials

Speculum

Bastard wing

Oystercatcher

Wing-bar

Rump

Terminal band

House sparrow (male)

Crown

Forehead

Beak

Ear coverts

Nape

Chin

Throat

Back

Breast

Rump

Upper tail coverts

Tail

Under tail coverts

Hind claw

Toes

Belly

Flanks

Tarsus

Supercilium

Eye-ring

Moustachial stripe

Reed bunting (female)

Naming the parts

Putting the right name to the parts of a bird is almost as important as naming the bird itself. For it provides a language in which to discuss birds with other birdwatchers, and it makes for quick and simple note-taking in the field.

view, and the first clues to the presence of a bird will almost certainly be sound – perhaps song, or the noise of scratching through dead leaves.

Do not be tempted at this point to move closer, because you will almost certainly frighten the bird away. Just wait and scan the trees and under-growth, and you will eventually see the source of the sound. If your presence is noticed and causes alarm, you will soon be aware of it; a noisy 'chack-chack-chack' is a good signal that it is time to move on.

As you walk through the woods, do not keep moving all the time, or you will see little evidence of birds. Make regular stops, for at least five minutes at a time, remaining motionless as before. Besides being less conspicuous, there is another motive for keeping still: in constant motion yourself, it is easy to miss the small movements in under-growth that can alert you to the presence of birdlife.

If you suspect that there are birds around, but they will not emerge from

What size is it?

When an unfamiliar bird is seen, the first point to note is its size. The easiest way to fix this is by comparing it with a bird that is known. Measured from its bill tip to the tip of its tail, for instance, a house sparrow is 5¾ in. (14·5 cm), while a blackbird is nearly twice as long, at 10 in. (25 cm). The familiar mallard is twice as long again, at 23 in. (58 cm), while its frequent companion on the waters of rivers and lakes, the mute swan, is the largest of all British birds, at 60 in. (152 cm) in length. The shape of a bird can also be very distinctive. For instance, it may be slim and delicate like a wagtail, or plump and stocky like a wood-pigeon.

House sparrow
5¾ in. (14·5 cm)
Heavily built,
with thick bill.

Blackbird
10 in. (25 cm)
Sturdy; adult
male's bill yellow.

Pied wagtail
7 in. (18 cm)
Long and slender.

Black-headed gull
15 in. (38 cm)
Long, pointed wings.

Wood-pigeon
16 in. (40 cm)
Heavy bodied;
broad wings.

Mallard
23 in. (58 cm)
Stout bodied;
long wings.

Mute swan
60 in. (152 cm)
Long neck, curved
when not in flight.

cover, try making a noise, but in the spring, do not go beating through the undergrowth – this could easily disturb breeding birds.

Evidence of birdlife is not always direct, and you can sometimes deduce much from the tell-tale traces that birds leave behind. Pellets on the ground beneath a tree indicate the location of an owl's favourite roost, and prominent bird-lime on a branch may well indicate a song-post.

Maps are of inestimable value when searching for new places to observe. The 1:50 000 Landranger series of Ordnance Survey maps mark woodland clearly, and indicate whether it is coniferous, deciduous or mixed.

A Garden for Birds

Watching birds in your own garden may seem mundane, but a remarkable range of species can be observed in even suburban gardens, particularly if there is woodland or water nearby. Indeed, you can do much to actually encourage birds into your garden – and not just by the obvious expedient of a bird-table.

THE BIRDS

An identification guide to 84 species

●

The species are grouped by family, starting with the more primitive families and ending with the most advanced species. For some basic advice on identifying birds, see pages 8-10; for further information on bird classification, see page 121.

●

If you already know the name of a species and want to look it it up, simply consult the index.

In flight, bold white wing-patches are visible. Fast-beating wings seem almost unable to support the long, drooping neck and body.

Double crest

Ruff

In winter plumage, white face and neck are conspicuous.

Juvenile has white head and neck, with black-brown streaks. Plumage is gradually moulted to winter plumage similar to that of adult.

Courting birds present vegetation and shake heads breast to breast.

Present all year; large lakes, south-west coasts in winter.

Adult bird in breeding plumage has double crest, ear-tufts, ruff and contrasting light and dark colouring. Boldly marked chicks are often carried by either parent. Sexes are alike. 19 in. (48 cm).

SITES GUIDE

The nest of the great crested grebe is often a floating platform of weeds, anchored among the reeds at the edge of a freshwater lake.

This bird is widespread, and can be seen at the majority of sites where there is fresh water – within the range indicated by the map on this page.

Great crested grebe *Podiceps cristatus*

Few British birds have a more elaborate and fascinating courtship display than the great crested grebe. Before the breeding season both sexes acquire conspicuous and beautiful dark head-plumes which are erected during the height of the courting display. This involves head-shaking, diving, fluffing out the plumage in the so-called 'cat' display, and presenting each other with water plants while rising from the water breast to breast. A century ago the fashion for ladies' grebe-feather hats meant that the birds were almost lost to Britain forever; but protection has since produced a large, healthy population.

The nest, like that of other grebes, is a simple heap of water plants built up from the bottom of shallows, or else supported by or tethered to a fallen branch or submerged stems. The shallow cup of the nest is surrounded by fine vegetable material which is used to cover the eggs when they are unattended.

The elongated, whitish eggs – usually four in number – take three and a half to four weeks to hatch into distinctively striped chicks. These squeak shrilly to the adults as they swim towards them to be fed on insects or fish. The chicks are dependent on the parents for at least ten weeks.

Location	Behaviour	Sketch
Date		
Time		
Weather	Field marks	
Call		

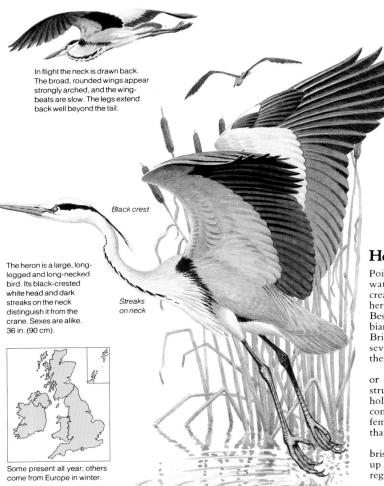

In flight the neck is drawn back. The broad, rounded wings appear strongly arched, and the wing-beats are slow. The legs extend back well beyond the tail.

Black crest

The heron is a large, long-legged and long-necked bird. Its black-crested white head and dark streaks on the neck distinguish it from the crane. Sexes are alike. 36 in. (90 cm).

Streaks on neck

Some present all year; others come from Europe in winter.

SITES GUIDE

In courtship display, the male heron may be seen stretching his neck up, then lowering it over his back.

The species may be seen at sites numbers: 1-3, 5, 7, 8, 10, 14, 19, 24-26, 28, 29, 32, 34, 37, 41, 42, 45, 47, 51-53.

Heron *Ardea cinerea*

Poised alert and motionless in or beside shallow water, the watchful heron waits patiently for a fish or some other small creature to come within range of its dagger-sharp bill. Then the heron strikes, stabbing the prey and swallowing it whole. Besides fish, herons readily take small mammals and amphibians, reptiles, insects and even birds. The heron population of Britain fluctuates between 4,000 and 4,500 pairs, but falls after severe winters when frozen rivers and lakes deprive the birds of their main food.

Herons nest in colonies, or heronries, building in large trees or bushes, in reed-beds or on cliff edges. The nest is a large structure of sticks and twigs with a shallow, saucer-shaped hollow in the top. The same nest is used year after year, and consequently grows in size until it is several feet across. The female usually builds the nest and lays three, four or five eggs that are pale greenish-blue in colour.

The chicks which emerge are clad in long, sparse down, bristly on the crown, giving a comical crest-like effect. Keeping up an incessant, begging 'agagagagag' call, they are fed by regurgitation by both parents.

Location	Behaviour	Sketch
Date		
Time		
Weather	Field marks	
Call		

Male mallards are often seen in pursuit of a female in flight.

In communal courtship displays, males pull their necks well back and often flick water with their bills.

When moulting, July–Sept., the flightless male resembles female, except for yellow bill.

Pairs often nest high in a waterside tree. Newly hatched ducklings have to drop to the ground.

Maroon breast

Green head

The adult female has a greenish-yellow bill and violet-blue wing-patch.

Present all year; many from west Europe winter in Britain.

Adult male has glossy green head, white collar, maroon breast and curly black tail-feathers. The mallard is the biggest of the surface-feeding ducks in the British Isles. 23 in. (58 cm).

SITES GUIDE

In winter mallards may be seen gathered around holes in the ice, in their search for food.

The species may be seen at sites numbers: 1, 2, 10, 14, 18, 21, 23-28, 34, 36, 37, 41-47, 49, 51-53.

Mallard *Anas platyrhynchos*

In both town and country, the mallard is the most familiar duck in the British Isles. It is as much at home on a park lake or city canal as it is on a quiet country backwater or remote reservoir. Mallards living near towns have learned to live side by side with man, often relying on him to supplement their diet with bread and other scraps of food. Country-dwelling birds, however, have learned to fear humans, because of the activities of wildfowlers.

The mallard is typical of the 'dabbling' ducks in that it feeds on the surface of the water and can spring straight up into the air with a powerful whirring of wings. Its broad, flattened bill is adapted for filtering from the water a wide range of tiny plant and animal matter. The webbed, paddle-like feet are placed well back on the mallard's body so that it walks with a rolling waddle from side to side.

The female mallard makes the quacking sound that people associate with ducks. The drake, however, also gives an occasional subdued, hoarse-sounding 'raarb' call, especially when suspicious or alarmed. Nests are made from leaves and grass, and lined with down. They are generally well-concealed.

Location	Behaviour	Sketch
Date		
Time		
Weather	Field marks	
Call		

Black head, neck

White chin-patch

Flightless like most wildfowl during the post-breeding moult, birds move first to safe waters.

Long neck and deep wing-beats are distinctive in flight.

Present all year; introduced species.

Aggressive displays include a threat posture with head lowered nearly to ground level.

Head and neck have unmistakable pattern. Sexes are alike. 36–40 in. (90–100 cm).

Juvenile bird has duller chin-patch and more mottled upper parts than adult; but first winter plumage resembles that of adult.

Sites Guide

The nest of the Canada Goose is a ground hollow lined with leaves, grass and down. The gander often stands guard.

The species may be seen at sites numbers: 14, 18, 24, 37, 41, 43, 45, 46.

Canada goose *Branta canadensis*

Extreme tameness has saved the Canada goose from becoming a popular target for wildfowlers and probably helped to give it the chance to establish itself as a wild breeding bird in Britain. The first Canada geese were brought across the Atlantic in the 17th century as decorative birds for parkland lakes. Attempts were later made to develop their numbers for shooting, but the bird is too tame, too irregular in its flighting times and flies too low to make it a 'sporting target'. It has now spread out of its parkland homes, and a countrywide census in 1976 revealed a population of more than 19,000 birds.

Although a large bird, the Canada goose can be unobtrusive when resting or feeding. Suddenly, however, a party may start calling with a trumpet-like honking. The noise builds up and the geese take wing, continuing their calls as they make for a neighbouring stretch of water.

The nest of the Canada goose consists of plant material at the water's edge or on an island. The female lays five or six creamy-white eggs in April or May. From these are hatched greenish-yellow or brown goslings. They can fly after nine weeks, but remain as a family until the following spring.

Location	Behaviour	Sketch
Date		
Time		
Weather	Field marks	
Call		

Female

Male

Flight is fast and direct, with neck and body outstretched to produce a long, narrow shape. White wing-patch is more extensive on male.

Double crest

Fishing birds often swim with head under water before submerging totally to dive on prey.

Red-brown breast

During its moult the male resembles the female, but back is darker and forewing whiter.

Adult female in breeding plumage has shorter crest than the male. The brown colouring of the head merges into neck and breast.

Present all year; mainly on estuaries in winter

Downy young are generally dark above and pale below, with white spots on their wings and backs.

Adult male has dark green head and reddish-brown breast and neck. Double crest and darker colouring distinguish it from goosander. 23 in. (58 cm).

Red-breasted merganser *Mergus serrator*

These ducks have a bad reputation among trout and salmon fishermen because of their taste for the young of the two fish. Defenders of the red-breasted merganser argue, however, that they also eat many non-game species, including eels, perch and pike which compete with or prey on the eggs or the young of salmon and trout.

The red-breasted merganser and the goosander are the only two species of sawbill duck that breed in the British Isles. They have finely serrated cutting edges to their bills that enable them to grasp slippery fish. The red-breasted merganser has a long history of residence in Scotland and Ireland. Since about 1950, however, in spite of some persecution, birds have spread into England, breeding as far south as Derbyshire, and also into Wales.

The nest is a shallow depression in the ground lined with grass, leaves and down. Thick vegetation usually makes it hard to find. From late April to early July the female lays and incubates eight to ten pale buff eggs that take a month to hatch. When the female leaves the nest, she camouflages the eggs with down. The ducklings can fly about two months after hatching.

Location	Behaviour	Sketch
Date		
Time		
Weather	Field marks	
Call		

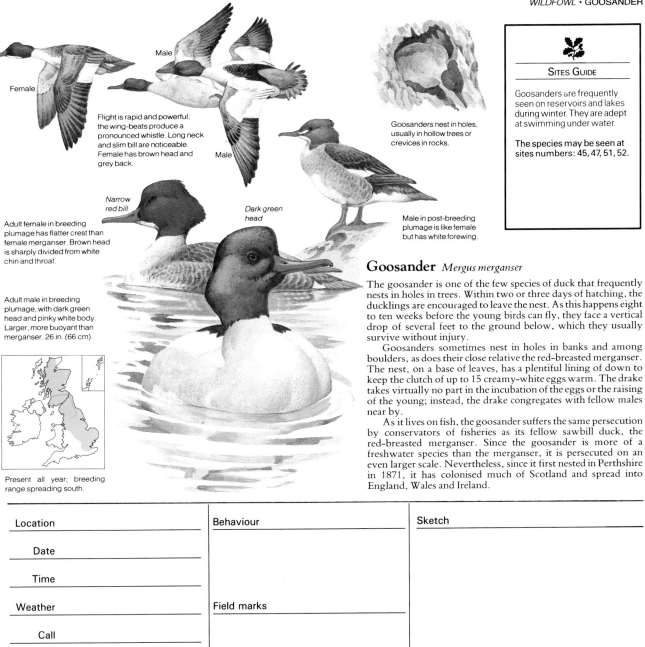

Female

Male

Flight is rapid and powerful; the wing-beats produce a pronounced whistle. Long neck and slim bill are noticeable. Female has brown head and grey back.

Male

Goosanders nest in holes, usually in hollow trees or crevices in rocks.

Narrow red bill

Dark green head

Adult female in breeding plumage has flatter crest than female merganser. Brown head is sharply divided from white chin and throat.

Adult male in breeding plumage, with dark green head and pinky white body. Larger, more buoyant than merganser. 26 in. (66 cm).

Male in post-breeding plumage is like female but has white forewing.

Present all year; breeding range spreading south.

Goosander *Mergus merganser*

The goosander is one of the few species of duck that frequently nests in holes in trees. Within two or three days of hatching, the ducklings are encouraged to leave the nest. As this happens eight to ten weeks before the young birds can fly, they face a vertical drop of several feet to the ground below, which they usually survive without injury.

Goosanders sometimes nest in holes in banks and among boulders, as does their close relative the red-breasted merganser. The nest, on a base of leaves, has a plentiful lining of down to keep the clutch of up to 15 creamy-white eggs warm. The drake takes virtually no part in the incubation of the eggs or the raising of the young; instead, the drake congregates with fellow males near by.

As it lives on fish, the goosander suffers the same persecution by conservators of fisheries as its fellow sawbill duck, the red-breasted merganser. Since the goosander is more of a freshwater species than the merganser, it is persecuted on an even larger scale. Nevertheless, since it first nested in Perthshire in 1871, it has colonised much of Scotland and spread into England, Wales and Ireland.

Location	Behaviour	Sketch
Date		
Time		
Weather	Field marks	
Call		

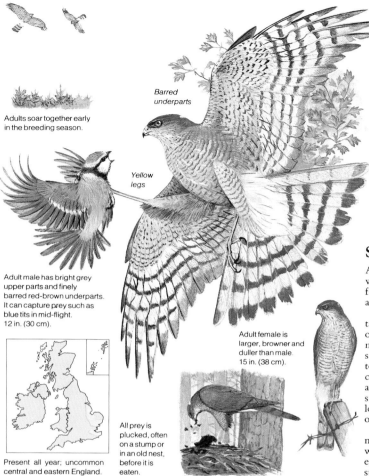

Barred
underparts

Adults soar together early
in the breeding season.

Yellow
legs

Adult male has bright grey
upper parts and finely
barred red-brown underparts.
It can capture prey such as
blue tits in mid-flight.
12 in. (30 cm).

Present all year; uncommon
central and eastern England.

All prey is
plucked, often
on a stump or
in an old nest,
before it is
eaten.

Adult female is
larger, browner and
duller than male.
15 in. (38 cm).

Short, rounded wings and long
tail are identifiable in flight.

Sites Guide

The sparrowhawk's nest is
made of sticks, especially
larch. It is lined with down
and twigs or pieces of bark.

The species may be seen at
sites numbers: 3, 4, 6, 7, 10,
11, 13, 15, 17-20, 23, 25-28,
31, 34, 36, 38, 40-43, 45, 47,
48, 50-53, 56, 57.

Sparrowhawk *Accipiter nisus*

Ambush is the sparrowhawk's favourite method of hunting. A watcher must be alert to spot the quick flurry and chorus of frantic alarm calls as the agile, yellow-eyed predator darts down a woodland ride or clearing, scattering terrified small birds.

Although most prey is probably captured with the advantage of surprise, the sparrowhawk is quite capable of outflying or overtaking its quarry with sheer superior power and skill, matching every twist and turn of its fleeing victim. Usually a small bird's only chance of escaping the long, slender yellow toes and their needle-sharp black talons is to dive into very dense cover. The short, rounded wings of the sparrowhawk are clearly adapted to woodland hunting; longer wings would not allow such nimble manoeuvring through the trees. Occasionally, a longer view of a sparrowhawk presents itself as it circles high over a wood – in search, perhaps, of a winter flock of finches.

The nest, a flattish, often bulky platform of sticks, is built mainly by the female. Sometimes the remains of a nest built by a wood pigeon or crow is used as a foundation. The three to six eggs are rounded and bluish-white, with spots, blotches and streaks of rich chocolate-brown.

Location	Behaviour	Sketch
Date		
Time		
Weather	Field marks	
Call		

Perching buzzard has an upright stance and shows a heavy, rounded build.

In gliding, wings are held flat with primary feathers turned back and pointed.

Wings are held forward and raised when soaring, with primary feathers turned up and tail widely spread.

Legs are unfeathered, unlike those of the visiting rough-legged buzzard.

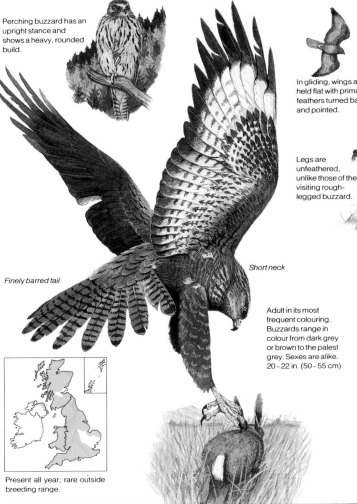

Short neck

Finely barred tail

Adult in its most frequent colouring. Buzzards range in colour from dark grey or brown to the palest grey. Sexes are alike. 20–22 in. (50–55 cm).

Present all year; rare outside breeding range.

Buzzard *Buteo buteo*

A familiar sound in hilly country in western or northern Britain is the mewing 'kiew' of a buzzard as it sails apparently without effort over a neighbouring hillside, circling in the updraught from the hill or in a rising thermal of hot air. The keen-sighted bird meanwhile scans the ground below for prey. Small mammals are its favourite food, in particular rabbits – so much so that the number of buzzards declined dramatically after myxomatosis almost wiped out Britain's rabbit population in the mid-1950s.

Buzzards prefer open hillsides and wooded valleys like those of South Wales, the Lake District and western Scotland; they are fewer in bare, mountainous regions and moorland. They build large nests of sticks or heather stalks and line them with finer twigs, bracken, grass, moss or seaweed.

The handsome eggs have a white or bluish-white shell decorated with brown spots or blotches. They take about a month to hatch, and since the eggs are laid at intervals of three or four days the young are of variable age. Young birds often die of starvation when food is short, but despite this, buzzards remain the most common of Britain's larger birds of prey.

Location	Behaviour	Sketch
Date		
Time		
Weather	Field marks	
Call		

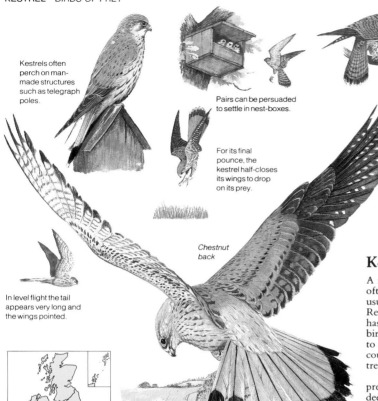

Kestrels often perch on man-made structures such as telegraph poles.

Pairs can be persuaded to settle in nest-boxes.

For its final pounce, the kestrel half-closes its wings to drop on its prey.

Female

Male

Young male's tail is grey, female's rusty-brown; both have dark bars.

Chestnut back

In level flight the tail appears very long and the wings pointed.

Present all year; our commonest bird of prey.

Adult male has chestnut back with grey head and tail. Kestrels hunt by searching while hovering; if no prey is seen the bird flies on, rises slightly, then hovers again. 13¼ in. (34 cm).

Grey tail with black band

SITES GUIDE

The natural sites for kestrels nests are tree cavities and disused crows' nests, though they also breed in buildings.

This bird is widespread, and may be seen at the majority of sites within the range indicated by the map on this page.

Kestrel *Falco tinnunculus*

A medium-sized, brownish bird hovering above the roadside is often a fleeting point of interest to the passing motorist and usually means imminent death for some small creature below. Reduced to low numbers in the late 1950s and 1960s, the kestrel has now largely recovered to become Britain's most widespread bird of prey. Its hovering technique of hunting – which gave rise to the country name of 'windhover' – can be watched in open countryside, along motorway verges and in urban areas. Kestrels have even nested in central London.

Typically, the kestrel flies along until prey or a likely spot for prey is sighted. It then checks and hovers, with occasional deeper wing-beats and tail fanned out and pointing down for stability. In spite of the exertion of hovering, the kestrel can keep its head motionless to pinpoint a possible meal. Lift-like, the bird drops by stages, finally pouncing and grasping with its talons. Small mammals are its staple diet.

Four or five rounded, heavily reddish-speckled eggs are incubated for about four weeks, mainly by the female. The chicks' coats of white down give way to brownish-grey before flight feathers develop. Chicks fly at four to five weeks.

Location	Behaviour	Sketch
Date		
Time		
Weather	Field marks	
Call		

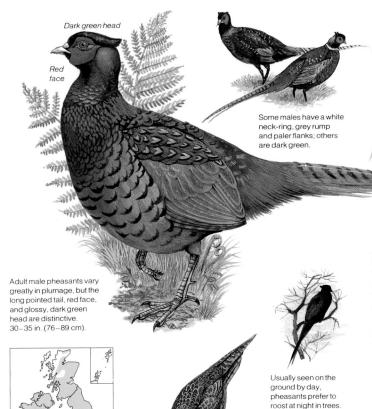

Dark green head

Red face

Some males have a white neck-ring, grey rump and paler flanks; others are dark green.

Though incapable of long-distance flight, pheasants can rise steeply and quickly when danger threatens.

Long, pointed tail

Adult male pheasants vary greatly in plumage, but the long pointed tail, red face, and glossy, dark green head are distinctive. 30–35 in. (76–89 cm).

Resident; breeds in heaths, hedges, reeds and woods.

Usually seen on the ground by day, pheasants prefer to roost at night in trees.

Adult female is smaller than male (21–25 in., 53–64 cm), mottled buff to blackish, and well camouflaged like the chicks.

SITES GUIDE

Pheasants forage in cultivated land for seeds and insects, but may also eat lizards, small snakes and mammals.

The species may be seen at sites numbers: 1, 4, 14, 16-19, 21, 23, 25, 26, 28, 34-38, 41-45, 47, 50-53.

Pheasant *Phasianus colchicus*

Though this colourful and handsome creature is Britain's most widespread game bird, it is not a native. The pheasant's natural home is in Asia, from the Caucasus eastwards to China. Its eating qualities were appreciated by the English in the early Middle Ages, when birds from the Caucasus were introduced. By the end of the 16th century they were common, and from late in the following century birds from China, distinguished by their white neck-rings, were being brought in.

In modern times, the large-scale rearing of pheasants in captivity for release to the wild has encouraged estate owners to maintain woods and copses on their land. This has brought some benefit to other forms of wildlife; on the other hand it has also led to the trapping and shooting of many species of mammals and birds which are regarded as special enemies of game birds, in spite of the protection given to them by the law.

For nesting, the pheasant favours almost any thick ground vegetation, though it prefers areas with trees as well. The nest, a shallow scrape in the ground, usually contains a clutch of 7–15 pale buff eggs. But the cock has several females in his 'harem', so a nest may contain more than one clutch.

Location	Behaviour	Sketch
Date		
Time		
Weather	Field marks	
Call		

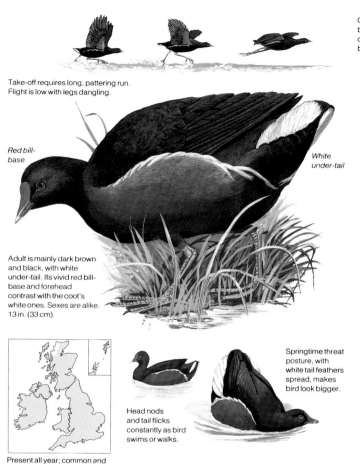

Take-off requires long, pattering run. Flight is low with legs dangling.

Red bill-base

White under-tail

Adult is mainly dark brown and black, with white under-tail. Its vivid red bill-base and forehead contrast with the coot's white ones. Sexes are alike. 13 in. (33 cm).

Present all year; common and widespread.

Head nods and tail flicks constantly as bird swims or walks.

Springtime threat posture, with white tail feathers spread, makes bird look bigger.

Chicks have bare blue crown and black down.

Juvenile is dull brown and pale-faced; tail pattern differs from coot's.

Moorhen *Gallinula chloropus*

In spite of its name, the moorhen is not a moorland bird; 'moor' comes from the Anglo-Saxon word *mor*, meaning mere or bog. The 16th-century naturalist William Turner called the bird 'mot-hen' because the species frequented 'moats which surround the houses of the great'. In fact, moorhens can be found on almost any stretch of fresh water.

The moorhen's food consists of water plants and their fruits and seeds, insects, spiders, worms and other invertebrates. Like the coot, the moorhen is aggressive in defence of its territory, and boundary disputes often lead to exchanges of blows with bill and feet. The moorhen's toes are particularly long, spreading its weight so that it can walk on floating water plants. There is no webbing between the toes, and perhaps because of this, the moorhen's swimming action seems laboured, the head jerking forward with each stroke like a cyclist toiling uphill. The bird swims readily under water, and when very alarmed stays submerged and motionless with only its bill above the surface.

One bird's clutch of eggs is likely to number five to ten, buff in colour with fine reddish-brown speckles. A nest may contain up to 20 eggs, laid by more than one female.

Location	Behaviour	Sketch
Date		
Time		
Weather	Field marks	
Call		

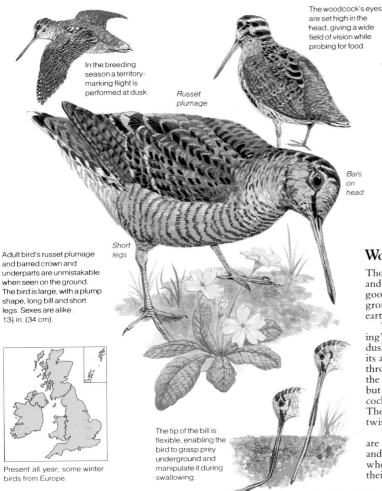

In the breeding season a territory-marking flight is performed at dusk.

Russet plumage

The woodcock's eyes are set high in the head, giving a wide field of vision while probing for food.

Bars on head

Adult bird's russet plumage and barred crown and underparts are unmistakable when seen on the ground. The bird is large, with a plump shape, long bill and short legs. Sexes are alike. 13½ in. (34 cm).

Short legs

When flushed from cover, the woodcock takes to the air and swerves adroitly among the trees to evade enemies.

Present all year; some winter birds from Europe.

The tip of the bill is flexible, enabling the bird to grasp prey underground and manipulate it during swallowing.

Woodcock *Scolopax rusticola*

Though it is a wader, the woodcock has deserted open marshes and taken to damp woodland with open clearings and rides and a good growth of bracken and bramble. Woodcocks need soft ground in which to feed, probing with their long bills for earthworms, insects and their larvae, centipedes and spiders.

The territorial display flight of the woodcock, called 'roding', is very distinctive. The male bird flies over its territory at dusk, covering a wide area on slow-beating wings which belie its actual speed of flight. From time to time it utters two calls, a throaty 'og-og-og' with the bill closed and a 'chee-wick' with the bill open. The first call is barely audible except at close range, but the second carries for a considerable distance. The woodcock's escape flight, when flushed from cover, is very different. Then it moves rapidly among the trees with deftly executed twists and turns.

The nest is a leaf–lined scrape in the ground. The eggs, which are pale fawn speckled with brown and grey, take between 20 and 23 days to hatch. The chicks are tended by both parents, and when danger threatens the parent birds usually squat and rely on their natural camouflage to prevent discovery.

Location	Behaviour	Sketch
Date		
Time		
Weather	Field marks	
Call		

Brown head

Dark red bill

Immature bird

Adult, winter

Wings have white fore-edge, black tips, all year. Immature birds have darkish band across wing.

Adult in breeding plumage. The 'black' head (in fact chocolate brown) is distinctive, as are the dark red bill and legs. Sexes are alike. 14–15 in. (36–38 cm).

Adult in winter: all that remains of the dark hood of its breeding plumage is a dark spot behind the eye.

Young birds have more grey in plumage than larger gull species at the same age.

SITES GUIDE

In southern Britain, inland sites such as reservoirs often hold colonies of black-headed gulls.

The species may be seen at sites numbers: 15, 26, 41, 43, 45, 47, 53.

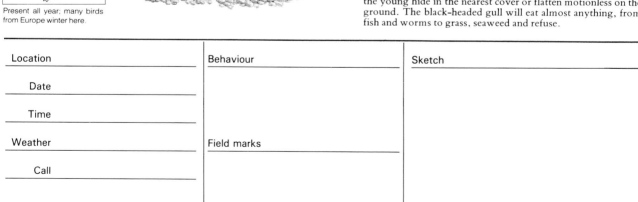

Flocks of birds follow ploughs and harrows to capture insects exposed in the turned-up soil.

Present all year; many birds from Europe winter here.

Black-headed gull *Larus ridibundus*

Of all the British gulls, the black-headed gull least deserves the description of 'sea-gull'. A recent survey showed that out of a total British population of some 300,000 pairs, only about a quarter nested on the coast. Meanwhile numerous colonies, some numbering many thousands of birds, were found inland, particularly in the north, usually in boggy areas around lakes.

In the south a higher proportion of colonies are on the coast, especially on salt marshes or among sand dunes. But even in the south the black-headed gull sometimes nests inland, on gravel or clay pits or on sewage farms.

The voice of the black-headed gull consists of a series of extremely harsh and rasping notes, and the sound of a colony in full cry is overpowering. The nest is a slight platform of vegetation or a sparsely lined scrape in the ground. There are normally three eggs, laid daily from mid-April onwards. Both parents incubate the eggs, for a total period of slightly more than three weeks. If danger threatens, the adults give the alarm and the young hide in the nearest cover or flatten motionless on the ground. The black-headed gull will eat almost anything, from fish and worms to grass, seaweed and refuse.

Location	Behaviour	Sketch
Date		
Time		
Weather	Field marks	
Call		

White neck-patch

Young birds lack the white neck-patch.

White on wings

In display flight the bird climbs steeply, claps its wings noisily then glides down again.

White wing-patches are conspicuous in flight. Take-off is marked by loud clatter of wings.

The largest of Britain's pigeons is distinguished by the white patch on its neck and the white wing-patches. Sexes are alike. 16 in. (40 cm).

Present all year; joined by some immigrants in winter.

Winter flocks in big numbers may raid crops such as kale.

Wood-pigeon *Columba palumbus*

In the eyes of farmers, the innocuous-looking wood-pigeon is undoubtedly 'public enemy number one' among British birds. Townsfolk find this hard to credit when they see the chubby, attractive bird quietly feeding in a local park. But in the country the wood-pigeon does immense damage to crops. It is particularly fond of cereals, potatoes, beans, peas and greens.

In winter, huge flocks of wood-pigeons feast upon root crops such as turnips, which are grown for animal feed, and clover, with which cereal crops are undersown. Without these modern 'additions' to the agricultural scene, the birds would have to fall back on their more traditional foods of ivy berries, acorns and weed seeds. Wood-pigeons are classified as pests and can be destroyed by the owners of the land where they nest.

The wood-pigeon's nest is a thin but well-built platform of fine twigs, through which the clutch of two pure white eggs can sometimes be seen from below. The newly born chicks are sparsely covered with yellowish down; but during their 29–35 days in the nest they develop their grey, juvenile plumage. The adult bird's voice is a delightful soft cooing, with the emphasis on the second of the usual five notes.

Location	Behaviour	Sketch
Date		
Time		
Weather	Field marks	
Call		

Adult stock dove in flight shows two short bars on each wing.

Grey rump

Rock dove
Columba livia

The rock dove in flight is distinguished from the stock dove by its bolder wing-bars, its white rump and its very long wings.

Stock doves and rock doves present all year.

The stock dove is a smaller bird than the wood-pigeon, lacking its white neck and wing markings. Each wing has two short bars; rump is grey. Sexes are alike. 13 in. (33 cm).

Two pairs of stock doves may fight for possession of a desirable nest-hole.

Stock dove *Columba oenas*

Holes in trees and rock faces and, very occasionally, disused rabbit burrows are the stock dove's favoured nesting places. The bird is found in both coastal and inland habitats – in parkland, woodland, and farmland with old trees; and also on cliffs. The nest itself may be merely a few plant fibres, twigs or roots on the floor of the hole; sometimes there is no lining at all.

Two pure white, fairly glossy eggs are usually laid sometime between late March and July – although clutches have been recorded from the beginning of March to October. Starting with the first egg, incubation is shared by both adults and lasts for 16–18 days. The chicks, or squabs as they are called, have rather sparse, coarse tufts of yellowish-brown down. They feed on a milky secretion from the lining of the parents' crops called pigeons' milk – which they take by thrusting their bills into the adults' throats.

The birds have a distinctive display flight, with two or more doves flying in circles and loops, often with wings raised and sometimes punctuated with wing-clapping. The rock dove – similar in general appearance to the stock dove – is found mostly on the coasts of Ireland and northern and western Scotland.

Location	Behaviour	Sketch
Date		
Time		
Weather	Field marks	
Call		

Courtship display postures include a bowing ritual performed in front of the female.

The frail nest of sticks is often built lower than those of other pigeons, and may be among brambles.

Reddish-brown upper parts are conspicuous in flight. From below, the tail appears black with a rounded white tip and the wings dusky.

Red-brown above

Black and white neck-patch

Pink breast

The turtle dove is a slender bird with chequered black and chestnut upper parts, and a black and white neck-patch. Sexes are alike. Up to 11 in. (28 cm).

Young bird is duller in colouring than adult, and lacks adult's neck-patch.

Apr.–Sept. visitor; has bred in Ireland.

Though the turtle dove is shyer than the collared dove, it will enter farmyards where grain is scattered to share it with poultry.

SITES GUIDE

Turtle dove nestlings – called squabs – have a covering of coarse, hair-like, straw-coloured down.

This bird is widespread, and may be seen at the majority of sites within the range indicated by the map on this page.

Turtle dove *Streptopelia turtur*

One of the most endearing bird calls of high summer is the musical, throbbing, purring coo of the turtle dove – 'poooorrr-poooorrr-poooorrr', the syllables repeated continuously in groups of two to five. It is a lazy, soporific sound, appropriate to the hot, hazy days on which it is so frequently heard. An attempt to represent this sound in the Latin species name *turtur* is the origin of the common name 'turtle' dove.

Turtle doves arrive in Britain from their winter quarters in sub-tropical Africa in the latter part of April and May, along with a few destined to move through to breeding grounds further on in northern Europe; they depart again from early August to the beginning of October. In between, some pairs will have succeeded in raising two broods of young. The nest is a flimsy, flat platform of thin twiglets and roots, occasionally incorporating other materials such as grass, rushes or hair.

Most clutches consist of two pinkish-white eggs, which are incubated by both male and female alternately for about two weeks. The chicks are fed by both parents with 'pigeons' milk', a soft, cheesy substance derived from the crop lining, and taken from the adults' throats by the thrusting bills of their offspring.

Location	Behaviour	Sketch
Date		
Time		
Weather	Field marks	
Call		

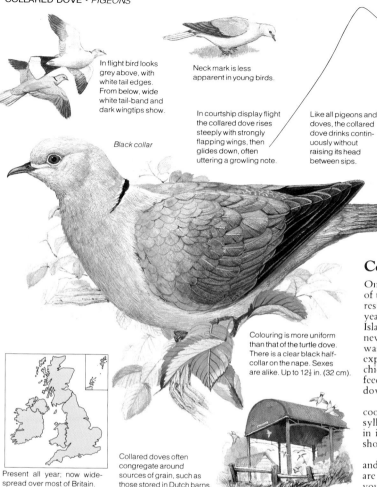

In flight bird looks grey above, with white tail edges. From below, wide white tail-band and dark wingtips show.

Neck mark is less apparent in young birds.

In courtship display flight the collared dove rises steeply with strongly flapping wings, then glides down, often uttering a growling note.

Like all pigeons and doves, the collared dove drinks continuously without raising its head between sips.

Black collar

Colouring is more uniform than that of the turtle dove. There is a clear black half-collar on the nape. Sexes are alike. Up to 12½ in. (32 cm).

Present all year; now widespread over most of Britain.

Collared doves often congregate around sources of grain, such as those stored in Dutch barns.

Sites Guide

The collared dove's nest, usually built in a tree, occasionally on buildings, is a thin, flat platform of twiglets and rootlets.

The species may be seen at sites numbers: 10, 19, 21, 25, 26, 35-37, 41, 43, 45, 47 and 51.

Collared dove *Streptopelia decaocto*

One of the most dramatic success stories in the bird world is that of the collared dove. Before about 1930 its European range was restricted to parts of the Balkans, but during the following 40 years the whole of Europe was colonised, as far as the Faeroe Islands and Iceland. By 1955 the bird was nesting in Britain. The new arrivals seemed to find an ecological niche that no other bird was filling, and having little competition, their population exploded. Favourite habitats were in the vicinity of farms, chicken runs, corn mills and docks, where grain or other animal feed were often spilled. In some areas, there are so many collared doves that they are treated as pests.

The bird's song is a reedy, hoarse-sounding 'cooo-cooooo-coo', with the emphasis on the middle syllable and the last syllable almost an afterthought. Though quite a pleasing sound in itself, it is repeated so frequently and regularly, with only short pauses, that it becomes extremely monotonous.

The breeding season is lengthy, some pairs starting in March and others rearing young as late as September. Only two eggs are laid in a clutch, but five broods may be raised in a year. The young spend three weeks in the nest.

Location	Behaviour	Sketch
Date		
Time		
Weather	Field marks	
Call		

Thin bill

Barred below

Apr.–Aug. visitor; widespread throughout Britain.

Adult bird in normal grey plumage. Underparts are lighter in colour than upper parts, and heavily barred. Tail is long and rounded, with white patches. Head is small and bill thin. Legs are yellow. Sexes are usually alike, but a few females are brown. 13 in. (33 cm).

Rounded tail

SITES GUIDE

The cuckoo's song inspired the 16th-century poet Edmund Spenser to write of 'The merry cuckoo, messenger of Spring'. It favours wooded areas.

This bird is widespread, and may be seen at the majority of sites within the range indicated by the map on this page.

Cuckoo *Cuculus canorus*

Each April the most eagerly awaited bird-call is that of the cuckoo, a sure sign that summer is on its way. The male bird announces his presence from a high perch and at great length, using the same monotonous but musical notes – 'coo-coo'. The female's call consists of an explosive, bubbling chuckle. Although mid-April is the likeliest time to hear the first cuckoo, some birds arrive from Africa towards the end of March.

The parasitic breeding habits of the cuckoo are notorious. From late May onwards the female flies over her chosen territory in search of foster-homes for her young. She selects a nest belonging to a pair of small birds – such as reed warblers – and deposits a single egg in it. Altogether, she may lay as many as 12 eggs in 12 different nests. Sometimes the eggs closely resemble those of the host bird: this is a natural adaptation and the female is not able to alter the colour and markings at will.

Since the mid-1940s there has been a widespread decrease in the cuckoo population. Reasons for this probably include the destruction of much of its habitat, including hedgerows; the increasing use of insecticides, which kill off its food; and the tendency towards colder, wetter, springs and summers.

Location	Behaviour	Sketch
Date		
Time		
Weather	Field marks	
Call		

When threatened, the adult bird flattens itself defensively on a barn floor, its wings spread horizontally. Its long-necked nestlings shelter behind it.

White face

Hollow elms are a favourite nest site with the barn owl, but they are fast disappearing from the countryside.

White underparts

Seen from above, the barn owl looks pure white. It systematically patrols fields at night in search of prey upon which to pounce.

Present all year; scarce in parts of eastern Britain.

Adult has white underparts, and golden-buff upper parts mottled with grey. It has a white heart-shaped face and long legs. Sexes are alike. 13½ in. (34 cm).

Sites Guide

The barn owl preys mainly on rats, mice and voles, which it usually hunts at night and carries off to its nest.

The species may be seen at sites numbers: 4, 5, 10, 14, 34, 36-38, 41, 43, 51, 52.

Barn owl *Tyto alba*

A barn owl's hoarse, eerie, prolonged shriek, often uttered in flight, still has the power to strike a chill into the hearts of those who recall the owl's reputation over the centuries as a bird of ill omen. Geoffrey Chaucer, in the 14th century, referred to the bird as a 'prophet of woe and mischance'.

Year after year many barn owls return to established roosts and breeding sites in old barns, ruins and exposed buildings such as church towers. The birds also inhabit natural holes in trees and cliffs. Often the location of these sites is revealed by large accumulations of castings or pellets, the indigestible remains of the birds' prey.

The breeding season is a long one, starting in February or March. Sometimes there are two broods. The size of each clutch of white eggs varies from three to 11, depending on the food available, but four to seven is the average. The male feeds the female during the 32–34 days of incubation. Young birds have two coats of down, the first white, the second, after 12 days, creamy. Like adult birds, the young make various hissing and snoring noises, but if disturbed in the nest they snap their bills together loudly. They fly at eight to ten weeks old.

Location	Behaviour	Sketch
Date		
Time		
Weather	Field marks	
Call		

Small birds often mob a tawny owl discovered in daylight, though they seldom succeed in disturbing their victim.

Recently fledged young still retain much of their barred downy underparts.

The owl watches for its prey from a tree perch, then swoops down in silent flight.

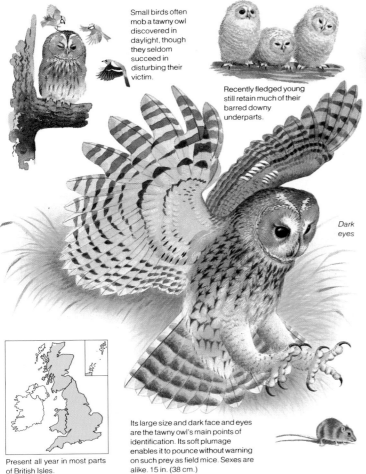

Dark eyes

Tawny owl *Strix aluco*

The call of the tawny owl is one of the best known of all bird songs. The familiar hoot, often described as 'to-whit-to-wooo', is really 'hoo-hoo-hoo . . . hoooooo': two or three short notes followed by a pause before the final quavering one. A less well-known call is the 'kee-wick' note, with a similar softer 'sheevick' uttered by the newly fledged young.

Owls are silent in flight because of their soft plumage and the comb-like leading edge to the wingtip. This allows the tawny owl to pounce from a perch, unheard by its prey. The bird's extraordinarily sensitive eyes and ears enable it to locate its prey in very dim light. Its diet consists largely of small mammals, but includes birds, frogs, fish, worms and large insects.

The tawny owl occurs in woodland and areas with scattered mature timber such as farmland, parklands and large gardens. Its nest is a shallow scrape in the bottom of a tree-hole or rock crevice, or very rarely a hole in the ground. Old nests of other birds are sometimes used. From about March onwards, the single clutch of one to seven rounded white eggs is laid at intervals of up to a week apart. Incubation starts with the first egg, so the young vary greatly in size.

Present all year in most parts of British Isles.

Its large size and dark face and eyes are the tawny owl's main points of identification. Its soft plumage enables it to pounce without warning on such prey as field mice. Sexes are alike. 15 in. (38 cm.)

Location	Behaviour	Sketch
Date		
Time		
Weather	Field marks	
Call		

The little owl's flight is low, swift and strongly undulating.

Yellow eyes

Fence posts and tree stumps are favourite day-time perches.

Its small size, yellow eyes and 'frowning' expression identify the little owl. Insects such as dor-beetles are its main prey. Sexes are alike. 8½ in. (22 cm).

Little owl *Athene noctua*

Warm spring evenings are the best time to listen for the call of the little owl: a long, musical but plaintive mewing 'kiew', repeated at widely spaced intervals. Occasionally the call is interspersed with a more excited, yelping 'werrrow'. The place to listen is on agricultural land where there are plenty of hollow trees and farm buildings, which provide nesting sites. Little owls can also be found in parkland, old orchards and quarries, and on sea cliffs.

The little owl was introduced to Britain from the Continent during the last century. By the early part of the 20th century it was widespread, breeding throughout most of England south of Yorkshire, except for the West Country. Wales was also partly colonised.

From mid-April onwards the single clutch of three to five eggs is laid on the bare floor of the nest cavity. The chicks hatch after about a month, and are at first clothed in thick, short, white down. Both adults feed them. They leave the nest often up to a week before they can fly well at five weeks old. The bird's diet consists largely of earthworms, molluscs and insects – particularly beetles – and some small mammals.

Present all year; derived from 19th-century introductions.

Fledgelings, when anxious, bob their heads in a comical manner.

Holes and crevices in old buildings are sometimes used as nesting sites. The eggs are incubated by the female.

Location	Behaviour	Sketch
Date		
Time		
Weather	Field marks	
Call		

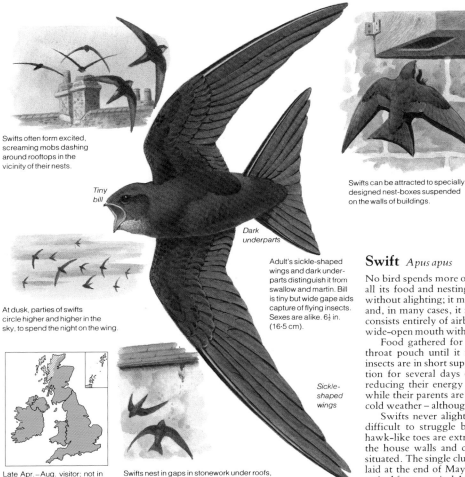

Swifts often form excited, screaming mobs dashing around rooftops in the vicinity of their nests.

Tiny bill

At dusk, parties of swifts circle higher and higher in the sky, to spend the night on the wing.

Dark underparts

Adult's sickle-shaped wings and dark underparts distinguish it from swallow and martin. Bill is tiny but wide gape aids capture of flying insects. Sexes are alike. 6½ in. (16·5 cm).

Sickle-shaped wings

Late Apr.–Aug. visitor; not in north-west Scotland.

Swifts nest in gaps in stonework under roofs, entering and leaving by narrow cracks.

Swifts can be attracted to specially designed nest-boxes suspended on the walls of buildings.

SITES GUIDE

The swifts' shallow nest is of fine plant material stuck together with their saliva. The young birds have pale feather edges.

This bird is widespread, and may be seen at the majority of sites within the range indicated by the map on this page.

Swift *Apus apus*

No bird spends more of its life in the air than the swift. It collects all its food and nesting material in flight; it drinks and bathes without alighting; it mates and can spend the night on the wing; and, in many cases, it manages to outfly birds of prey. Its food consists entirely of airborne insects which are funnelled into its wide-open mouth with the help of the surrounding stiff bristles.

Food gathered for the young is accumulated in the bird's throat pouch until it forms a large, compacted bulge. When insects are in short supply, the chicks can survive partial starvation for several days or even weeks by becoming torpid, so reducing their energy loss. Before their feathers develop, and while their parents are out hunting, they can even survive quite cold weather – although they become sluggish at such times.

Swifts never alight on the ground voluntarily, and find it difficult to struggle back into the air if they do. But their hawk-like toes are extremely strong, enabling them to cling to the house walls and cliff faces on which their nest holes are situated. The single clutch of two or three smooth, white eggs is laid at the end of May or the beginning of June, on the adults' arrival from tropical Africa.

Location	Behaviour	Sketch
Date		
Time		
Weather	Field marks	
Call		

Grey-brown plumage

Adult male has soft, grey-brown plumage. Slow beating of long wings is characteristic. Bill is small, but as it is opened, lower jaw becomes wider, giving wide gape for catching insects. 10½ in. (27 cm).

Wide gape

When perching, bird is usually aligned along the branch rather than across it.

Nightjars are usually seen in flight at dusk, gliding and banking erratically but buoyantly.

May – Oct. visitor; commonest East Anglia and the south.

Female lacks white wing-spots and tail-spots of male. The nest is no more than a scrape in the ground.

Nightjar *Caprimulgus europaeus*

Its extraordinary churring-jarring song, heard mostly at night, gives the nightjar its name. The sound is rather like that of a small engine revving rapidly for stretches of up to five minutes, with an alternating rise and fall in pitch. During this performance, the bird is usually perched lengthwise along a dead branch – though it sometimes delivers its song from a leafy branch, or even from the ground or in flight. By contrast, the call note is a simple 'cooic'.

On arriving from the southern half of Africa in the spring, the nightjar takes up territory in open woodland, heathland, moorland or coastal sand-dunes. During the day, the birds are almost invisible as they lie motionless on the ground and, from a distance, they are often mistaken for bunches of dead leaves. They lay their eggs on bare ground, often near dead wood, and this makes a sitting bird even harder to see.

The clutch of two eggs is laid from about mid-May onwards. Both parents take part in incubation, but the hen only does so during the day. Both birds feed the chicks until the female starts to incubate her second clutch, when the male manages alone. After dusk, the nightjar feeds on flying insects.

Location	Behaviour	Sketch
Date		
Time		
Weather	Field marks	
Call		

In flight, the green woodpecker's yellowish rump is its most striking feature.

Red crown

Juvenile

Green back

Female

Adult female has black moustache. Juveniles have pale-spotted upper parts and streaked underparts.

Adult bird's green back and red crown are distinctive. Male has a red moustache. Stiff tail feathers act as a prop while climbing. 12½ in. (32 cm).

Present all year; spreading in Scotland since 1951.

Sites Guide

The green woodpecker may sometimes perch on a branch in the water. It favours meadows, woods and parks.

This bird is widespread, and may be seen at the majority of sites within the range indicated by the map on this page.

Green woodpecker *Picus viridis*

In some country areas the green woodpecker, largest of Britain's woodpeckers, is known as the 'yaffle' – an allusion to the bird's attractive, loud laughing call. This takes the form of a rapidly repeated 'kew-kew-kew . . .', fairly high-pitched at first, then falling. The green woodpecker seldom indulges in the 'drumming' action of the other species. It also feeds much more on the ground, for besides larvae of wood-boring insects, beetles, moths and flies, it is particularly partial to ants and their grubs. The bird has also been known to damage hives in search of bees and their grubs.

During courtship, the green woodpecker performs the same spiral pursuits round branches as the greater spotted woodpecker. However, the green species has one display all of its own; males fighting over a female sway their heads from side-to-side, with wings spread, tails fanned and crests raised. Only one brood is produced each year. Usually, five to seven eggs are laid in a bare nesting chamber, but clutches of up to 11 eggs have been known. Both sexes share in incubating the eggs for 18–19 days, and in feeding the young for 18–21 days by regurgitating a milky paste produced from their insect food.

Location	Behaviour	Sketch
Date		
Time		
Weather	Field marks	
Call		

Starlings often appropriate woodpeckers' nests.

In flight, the great spotted woodpecker's white shoulder patches are easily recognised.

The bird sometimes makes aerial sorties, like a flycatcher, to take insects on the wing.

Female

White shoulder

A nest hole in a tree, usually at least 10 ft (3 m) above the ground, is excavated by the male and female together.

Juveniles have a red cap like the adult male lesser spotted woodpecker, and have white shoulder patches.

Red under-tail covert

Present all year; migrants may reach Ireland.

Its larger size, red under tail covert and white shoulder patches distinguish the great spotted woodpecker from the lesser spotted. Male has red nape-patch, which female lacks. 9 in. (23 cm).

Great spotted woodpecker *Dendrocopos major*

A characteristic 'drumming' often gives away the presence of a great spotted woodpecker. The sound is made by rapid blows of the bill on some resonant surface such as a dead bough or a telegraph pole. Both sexes do this, as a means of proclaiming ownership of territory, and each 'drum' consists of some eight to ten blows delivered within the space of a single second. The bird also has an unmistakable call, a far-carrying 'tchick'.

Sometimes known as the pied woodpecker because of its mainly black and white plumage, the great spotted woodpecker is much larger than the lesser spotted but smaller than the green woodpecker. It is more a woodland bird than the other two, living in both coniferous and deciduous woods. However, since about 1950 it has spread into towns and suburban parks and gardens.

The bird indulges in elaborate courtship displays. The male will frequently make spiral pursuits of a female round tree branches, and a mutual display flight involves short, quivering wing-beats from tree to tree. The female does the major share of the 16 or so days' incubation of the pure white, glossy eggs, but both parents feed the chicks – on insects brought in the bill.

Location	Behaviour	Sketch
Date		
Time		
Weather	Field marks	
Call		

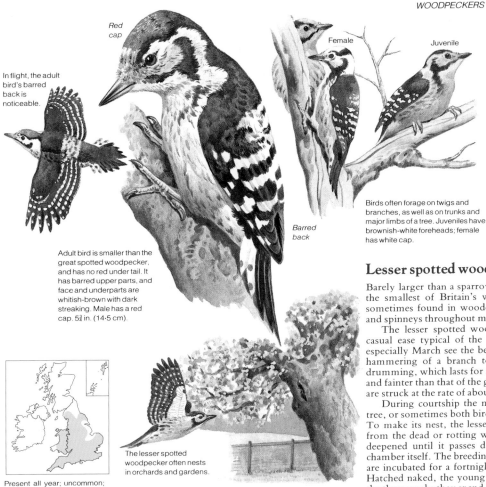

Red cap

In flight, the adult bird's barred back is noticeable.

Female

Juvenile

Adult bird is smaller than the great spotted woodpecker, and has no red under tail. It has barred upper parts, and face and underparts are whitish-brown with dark streaking. Male has a red cap. 5¾ in. (14·5 cm).

Barred back

Birds often forage on twigs and branches, as well as on trunks and major limbs of a tree. Juveniles have brownish-white foreheads; female has white cap.

The lesser spotted woodpecker often nests in orchards and gardens.

Present all year; uncommon; most numerous in south.

SITES GUIDE

Lesser spotted woodpeckers may be seen in May or June bringing insect larvae to feed their young.

The species may be seen at sites numbers: 3, 4, 6, 10, 11, 14, 16, 18, 19, 22, 25-28, 31, 34, 36-41, 43, 45-47, 53.

Lesser spotted woodpecker *Dendrocopos minor*

Barely larger than a sparrow, the lesser spotted woodpecker is the smallest of Britain's woodpeckers. It is an elusive bird, sometimes found in wooded gardens, old orchards, parkland and spinneys throughout much of England and Wales.

The lesser spotted woodpecker climbs up trees with the casual ease typical of the woodpecker family. February and especially March see the beginning of 'drumming' – the rapid hammering of a branch to establish territory. Each spell of drumming, which lasts for about two seconds, is usually longer and fainter than that of the great spotted woodpecker; the blows are struck at the rate of about 15 per second.

During courtship the male flutters moth-like from tree to tree, or sometimes both birds sit rigidly side by side on a bough. To make its nest, the lesser spotted woodpecker pecks a hole from the dead or rotting wood. The hole is then widened and deepened until it passes down inside the branch to the nest chamber itself. The breeding season is lengthy, and eggs, which are incubated for a fortnight, may be laid from April to June. Hatched naked, the young grow their juvenile feathers during the three weeks they spend in the nest.

Location	Behaviour	Sketch
Date		
Time		
Weather	Field marks	
Call		

Russet throat

Male

Female

Adult male's russet throat and long tail streamers are unmistakable. Upper parts are bluish-black, and there are white spots on the tail. Adult female has shorter tail streamers and is generally duller. 7½ in. (19 cm).

Long tail streamers

Mar.–Oct. visitor; widespread; none in cities.

SITES GUIDE

The swallow's nest is a cup of mud with straw to bind it together, lined with feathers and placed on a ledge or against a roof beam or similar support.

This bird is widespread, and may be seen at the majority of sites within the range indicated by the map on this page.

Swallow *Hirundo rustica*

The old country saying that 'one swallow doesn't make a summer' is more justified than many of its kind. For although the swallow is popularly regarded as a harbinger of summer, the first birds may appear from their South African wintering grounds as early as the beginning of March. Adult birds usually return to the same locality where they bred the previous year – often to exactly the same site. Throughout the summer breeding season the swallow's pleasant twittering warble may be heard well before sunrise, from a bird in flight or from a perch.

When men lived in caves swallows probably did the same; nowadays they have adapted to nesting in buildings and under bridges. Usually, each of the two or three clutches produced in a year consists of three to six eggs, glossy white with a speckling of pinkish-brown or pale grey.

In autumn, adults and young birds head for the South African sun, feeding off insects caught on the wing. It was once thought that when swallows disappeared in autumn they had buried themselves in the mud of rivers and ponds: an idea doubtless fostered by the fact that the birds often congregate in such places just before they migrate.

Location

Date

Time

Weather

Call

Behaviour

Field marks

Sketch

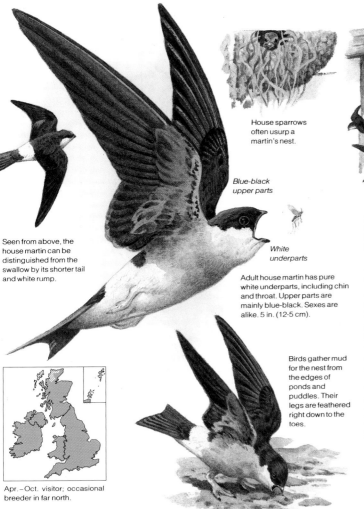

House sparrows often usurp a martin's nest.

Blue-black upper parts

White underparts

Seen from above, the house martin can be distinguished from the swallow by its shorter tail and white rump.

Adult house martin has pure white underparts, including chin and throat. Upper parts are mainly blue-black. Sexes are alike. 5 in. (12·5 cm).

Birds gather mud for the nest from the edges of ponds and puddles. Their legs are feathered right down to the toes.

Apr.–Oct. visitor; occasional breeder in far north.

Dense colonies may be found under sheltering roof eaves, the birds constantly coming and going with characteristic flicking of wings.

SITES GUIDE

Young house martins remain in the nest for about three weeks until very fully developed. Both parents feed them.

The species may be seen at sites numbers: 3-5, 7, 10, 14, 16, 20, 21, 25, 26, 28, 33, 36, 37, 41-43, 45, 47, 53.

House martin *Delichon urbica*

A masterpiece in mud, the house martin's nest is snug and flask-shaped with only a small entrance near the top at one side. It is commonly built just under the eaves of a house. The mud pellets are taken up in beakfuls by both male and female and reinforced with plant fibres. Traditionally the house martin is a cliff-nesting species, and although there are still a few cliff colonies to be found, the bird has happily adapted itself to the convenient sites offered by man-made buildings.

Breeding starts towards the end of May, a few weeks after the birds arrive from their African wintering quarters. The nest is lined with dried grass, other plant material and feathers before the female lays a clutch of four or five glossy white eggs. These hatch in 13–19 days, and the young birds spend three or three and a half weeks in the nest before they are ready to fly from it. Two or three broods may be reared each year, and sometimes young birds from an earlier brood help feed later ones.

House martins feed on insects on the wing, swooping and wheeling in pursuit. Their call is a series of chirrups and twitters, with a 'tseep' alarm note. The song, like the quieter notes of a budgerigar, is uttered in flight, from a perch or inside the nest.

Location	Behaviour	Sketch
Date		
Time		
Weather	Field marks	
Call		

Crest

Buff eye-stripes

In flight, white wing marks, dark outer tail feathers and white nape band distinguish the woodlark from the skylark.

The bird usually delivers its mellow song in a circular song flight.

Short tail

Woodlark has shorter tail and more richly patterned plumage than skylark, and has buffish eye-stripes meeting across the nape. There is a small crest. Sexes are alike. 6 in. (15 cm).

Partial migrant; scarce, decreased in recent years.

Normally the woodlark feeds on insects, but in autumn it eats seeds.

SITES GUIDE

The woodlark's nest is a neat cup of grass, moss and roots built on the ground and lined with horsehair and other fine material.

The species may be seen at sites numbers: 3, 4, 23, 26, 45, 47.

Woodlark *Lullula arborea*

The song of the woodlark is highly distinctive – a rich, sweet, mellow medley, consisting of varied phrases of one or more notes repeated several times, and interspersed with an occasional 'loo-loo-loo', from which the bird's generic name is derived. The song is delivered from a tree or bush, or during the song flight. In this, the male spirals higher and higher in wide circles, then gradually drops back. Occasionally the bird falls silent at about 100 ft, then plummets with closed wings almost to the ground, opening its wings as brakes just before it alights. Although a bird of open terrain, like the skylark, the woodlark favours land with scattered trees.

Three or four eggs are laid, usually in early April. They are similar in colour to those of the skylark. Incubation takes 12–16 days. Both parents feed the chicks, which leave the nest after 11–12 days, a few days before they can fly properly.

At the beginning of the 19th century, woodlarks were said to breed in virtually every county in England and Wales, but now they are scarce. The cold winters of 1961–2 and 1962–3 decimated them. More recent declines may be due to loss of habitat through afforestation and more intensive agriculture.

Location	Behaviour	Sketch
Date		
Time		
Weather	Field marks	
Call		

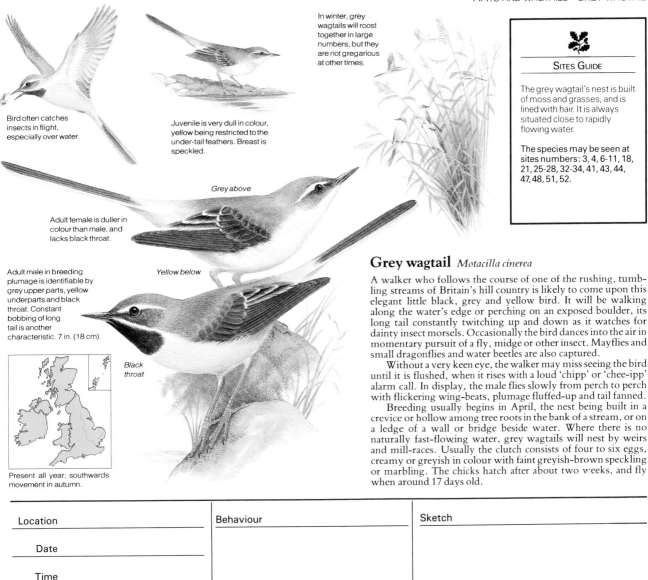

In winter, grey wagtails will roost together in large numbers, but they are not gregarious at other times.

Bird often catches insects in flight, especially over water.

Juvenile is very dull in colour, yellow being restricted to the under-tail feathers. Breast is speckled.

Grey above

Adult female is duller in colour than male, and lacks black throat.

Yellow below

Adult male in breeding plumage is identifiable by grey upper parts, yellow underparts and black throat. Constant bobbing of long tail is another characteristic. 7 in. (18 cm).

Black throat

Present all year; southwards movement in autumn.

SITES GUIDE

The grey wagtail's nest is built of moss and grasses, and is lined with hair. It is always situated close to rapidly flowing water.

The species may be seen at sites numbers: 3, 4, 6-11, 18, 21, 25-28, 32-34, 41, 43, 44, 47, 48, 51, 52.

Grey wagtail *Motacilla cinerea*

A walker who follows the course of one of the rushing, tumbling streams of Britain's hill country is likely to come upon this elegant little black, grey and yellow bird. It will be walking along the water's edge or perching on an exposed boulder, its long tail constantly twitching up and down as it watches for dainty insect morsels. Occasionally the bird dances into the air in momentary pursuit of a fly, midge or other insect. Mayflies and small dragonflies and water beetles are also captured.

Without a very keen eye, the walker may miss seeing the bird until it is flushed, when it rises with a loud 'chipp' or 'chee-ipp' alarm call. In display, the male flies slowly from perch to perch with flickering wing-beats, plumage fluffed-up and tail fanned.

Breeding usually begins in April, the nest being built in a crevice or hollow among tree roots in the bank of a stream, or on a ledge of a wall or bridge beside water. Where there is no naturally fast-flowing water, grey wagtails will nest by weirs and mill-races. Usually the clutch consists of four to six eggs, creamy or greyish in colour with faint greyish-brown speckling or marbling. The chicks hatch after about two weeks, and fly when around 17 days old.

Location	Behaviour	Sketch
Date		
Time		
Weather	Field marks	
Call		

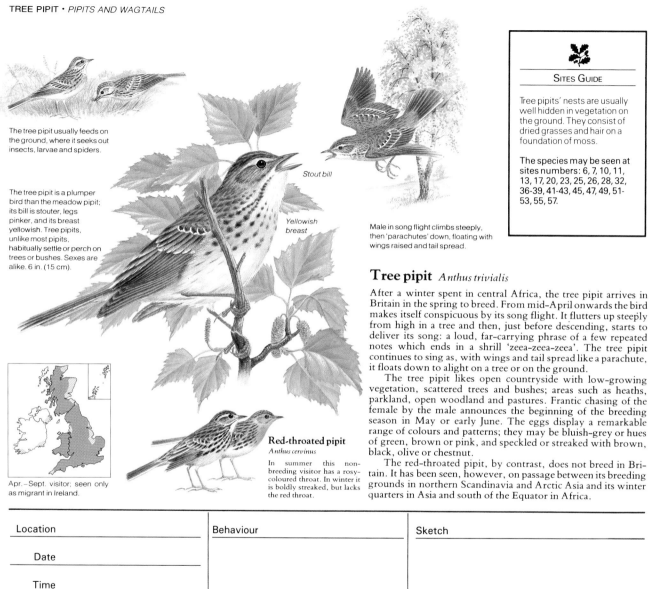

The tree pipit usually feeds on the ground, where it seeks out insects, larvae and spiders.

The tree pipit is a plumper bird than the meadow pipit; its bill is stouter, legs pinker, and its breast yellowish. Tree pipits, unlike most pipits, habitually settle or perch on trees or bushes. Sexes are alike. 6 in. (15 cm).

Stout bill

Yellowish breast

Male in song flight climbs steeply, then 'parachutes' down, floating with wings raised and tail spread.

Apr.–Sept. visitor; seen only as migrant in Ireland.

Red-throated pipit
Anthus cervinus

In summer this non-breeding visitor has a rosy-coloured throat. In winter it is boldly streaked, but lacks the red throat.

SITES GUIDE

Tree pipits' nests are usually well hidden in vegetation on the ground. They consist of dried grasses and hair on a foundation of moss.

The species may be seen at sites numbers: 6, 7, 10, 11, 13, 17, 20, 23, 25, 26, 28, 32, 36-39, 41-43, 45, 47, 49, 51-53, 55, 57.

Tree pipit *Anthus trivialis*

After a winter spent in central Africa, the tree pipit arrives in Britain in the spring to breed. From mid–April onwards the bird makes itself conspicuous by its song flight. It flutters up steeply from high in a tree and then, just before descending, starts to deliver its song: a loud, far-carrying phrase of a few repeated notes which ends in a shrill 'zeea-zeea-zeea'. The tree pipit continues to sing as, with wings and tail spread like a parachute, it floats down to alight on a tree or on the ground.

The tree pipit likes open countryside with low-growing vegetation, scattered trees and bushes; areas such as heaths, parkland, open woodland and pastures. Frantic chasing of the female by the male announces the beginning of the breeding season in May or early June. The eggs display a remarkable range of colours and patterns; they may be bluish–grey or hues of green, brown or pink, and speckled or streaked with brown, black, olive or chestnut.

The red-throated pipit, by contrast, does not breed in Britain. It has been seen, however, on passage between its breeding grounds in northern Scandinavia and Arctic Asia and its winter quarters in Asia and south of the Equator in Africa.

Location	Behaviour	Sketch
Date		
Time		
Weather	Field marks	
Call		

In summer, adults of both sexes have yellow bills and shining black plumage shot with purple and green. Throat feathers are raised during song from a prominent perch. 8½ in. (22 cm).

Iridescent plumage

Yellow bill

Flight is straight and fast, but birds wheel and glide when pursuing insects.

Nests are often in old woodpecker holes, but any hole in a tree, wall or cliff will do. Males begin the nest before pairing.

After breeding, starlings often gather in flocks of thousands, calling noisily before settling to roost.

Present all year; migrants swell winter numbers.

Juveniles are mouse-brown. They slowly develop winter adult plumage – black with white spots, which are more pronounced in the female.

Adult in winter plumage probes for food with open bill.

Starling *Sturnus vulgaris*

In town or country the starling is as familiar as weeds in a garden and often just as unwelcome. Brash, aggressive and a ruthless opportunist – it is the tearaway of the bird-world – a noisy swaggerer that bullies other birds on feeding grounds, fouls buildings with its droppings and fills the air with its high-pitched squealing as it flocks on ledges and in high trees.

Thousands of starlings are present in Britain all the year round, and between the end of September and April their numbers are swollen by millions more that come from the Continent to take advantage of the mild winter climate. In areas where flocks numbering hundreds of thousands congregate they can strip farmlands bare of corn; on the other hand, they also eat leatherjackets, wireworms and other agricultural pests.

Starlings start to breed from mid-April. The nest is an untidy accumulation of grass, straw and leaves in which are laid five to seven light blue eggs which take 12 to 15 days to hatch. The young are as noisy as adult birds, clamouring incessantly for food and pestering their parents for some time after leaving the nest. The starling's song is a jumble of squeaks and whistles, and it is an expert mimic of other birds.

Location	Behaviour	Sketch
Date		
Time		
Weather	Field marks	
Call		

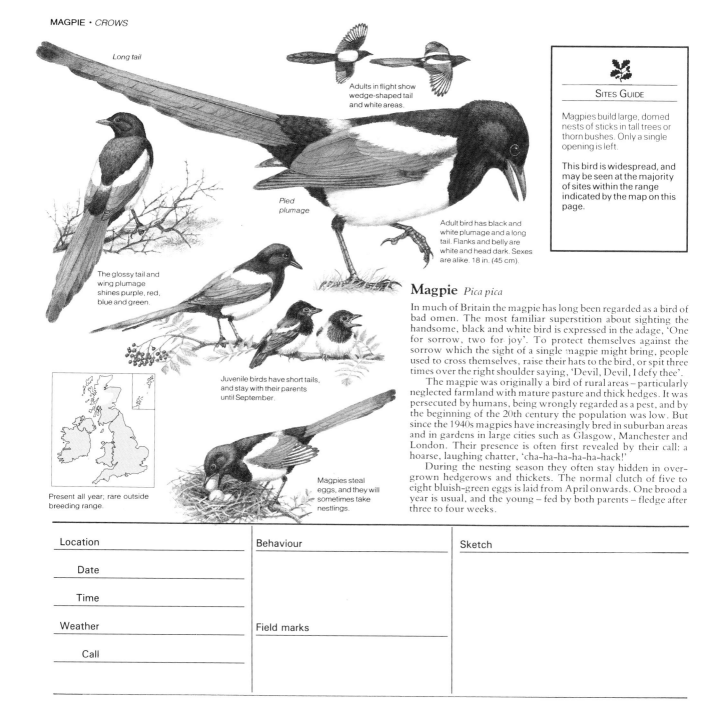

Long tail

Adults in flight show wedge-shaped tail and white areas.

Pied plumage

The glossy tail and wing plumage shines purple, red, blue and green.

Adult bird has black and white plumage and a long tail. Flanks and belly are white and head dark. Sexes are alike. 18 in. (45 cm).

Juvenile birds have short tails, and stay with their parents until September.

Magpies steal eggs, and they will sometimes take nestlings.

Present all year; rare outside breeding range.

SITES GUIDE

Magpies build large, domed nests of sticks in tall trees or thorn bushes. Only a single opening is left.

This bird is widespread, and may be seen at the majority of sites within the range indicated by the map on this page.

Magpie *Pica pica*

In much of Britain the magpie has long been regarded as a bird of bad omen. The most familiar superstition about sighting the handsome, black and white bird is expressed in the adage, 'One for sorrow, two for joy'. To protect themselves against the sorrow which the sight of a single magpie might bring, people used to cross themselves, raise their hats to the bird, or spit three times over the right shoulder saying, 'Devil, Devil, I defy thee'.

The magpie was originally a bird of rural areas – particularly neglected farmland with mature pasture and thick hedges. It was persecuted by humans, being wrongly regarded as a pest, and by the beginning of the 20th century the population was low. But since the 1940s magpies have increasingly bred in suburban areas and in gardens in large cities such as Glasgow, Manchester and London. Their presence is often first revealed by their call: a hoarse, laughing chatter, 'cha-ha-ha-ha-ha-hack!'

During the nesting season they often stay hidden in overgrown hedgerows and thickets. The normal clutch of five to eight bluish-green eggs is laid from April onwards. One brood a year is usual, and the young – fed by both parents – fledge after three to four weeks.

Location	Behaviour	Sketch
Date		
Time		
Weather	Field marks	
Call		

Nutcracker
Nucifraga caryocatactes
Another member of the crow family, this thin-billed bird has a brown body with bold white spots. In flight, its white under-tail and terminal band are conspicuous. 12¼ in. (32 cm).

Rump and wing pattern is conspicuous in the jay's wave-like flight. It usually stays near trees.

Streaked crest

The jay sometimes steals nestlings and eggs of other birds, such as blackbirds.

Adult bird has buff body with white rump, distinctive blue wing-patch, blue eyes and streaked crest. Sexes are alike. 13½ in. (34 cm).

Blue wing-patch

The jay is fond of acorns which it collects and buries among fallen leaves and twigs.

Present all year; sedentary, with some immigrants.

SITES GUIDE

The jay's nest is usually situated in a tree and is made of twigs bound with earth and lined with hair.

This bird is widespread, and may be seen at the majority of sites within the range indicated by the map on this page.

Jay *Garrulus glandarius*

As one of Britain's most wary birds, the jay is more often heard than seen. It greets woodland 'intruders' with a raucous, scolding call of 'scaaarg-scaaarg'. The jay is sometimes observed hopping along the ground and picking up seeds or acorns from under trees. When spotted in flight, it is usually flitting from one group of trees to another with distinctive, jerky beats of its rounded wings.

Jays depend heavily upon trees – especially oaks – for their existence. They bury acorns for their winter food and also store beech-nuts, peas, potatoes, fruit and berries. To a lesser extent, they eat small mammals, molluscs, earthworms, spiders and the eggs and young of other birds.

In the spring, the birds sometimes hold formal courtship ceremonies, in which groups of jays pursue each other with slow wing-beats and a great deal of calling. The ceremonies often speed up and reach their climax in an excited chase through the branches of trees, during which the male birds turn their bodies sideways to the females and raise their crest and body feathers. Usually five to seven eggs are laid and hatch in about two weeks. The young spend about three weeks in the nest.

Location	Behaviour	Sketch
Date		
Time		
Weather	Field marks	
Call		

Jackdaws sometimes hover in the air showing darkish bands under wings, and dark grey tail.

Grey nape

Dark grey underparts

Birds flock together, and have a liking for derelict buildings.

This small member of the crow family is easily identified by its grey nape and dark grey underparts. Other plumage is black. Sexes are alike. 13 in. (33 cm).

A jackdaw nesting in a chimneypot can be an unwelcome visitor; after years of use, the nest sticks may block the chimney.

Jackdaw *Corvus monedula*

The thieving habits of the jackdaw were celebrated by the early 19th-century humorous poet Richard Harris Barham in *The Jackdaw of Rheims.* In the poem the bird – the most notorious robber in the crow family – steals the ring of the Cardinal Lord Archbishop of Rheims. 'The Devil,' wrote Barham, 'must be in that little Jackdaw.' Apart from snatching and hiding such inedible objects, the jackdaw occasionally steals young birds and eggs which it adds to its diet of seeds, fruit, insects and carrion.

As well as nesting in holes and chimneys, the jackdaw sometimes takes over the old nests of other birds, and occasionally even makes its nest in a rabbit burrow. The amount of nest material used depends very much upon the site. A large, exposed nest is usually lined with hair, fur, grass and wool – which the jackdaw sometimes plucks from the backs of sheep.

Late April sees the start of the breeding season, and three to seven eggs with black and grey speckles are laid. Incubation is by the female who is fed on the nest by the male. The young hatch in 17–18 days and are ready to fledge when about one month old. Usually, the jackdaw's call is a loud, explosive 'tchack'; occasionally this is expanded into a 'tchackertchack'.

A hole in a tree trunk is a favourite nesting place.

Present all year; winter immigrants from Continent.

The jackdaw is a sociable bird, which often feeds with birds of other species.

Location	Behaviour	Sketch
Date		
Time		
Weather	Field marks	
Call		

Face-patch

A bare face-patch distinguishes the rook from the carrion crow, and gives a long-billed appearance. Plumage is black with a purple gloss; thigh feathers are thick. Sexes are alike. 18 in. (45 cm).

In breeding season, adults carry food to young in a throat pouch.

Thigh feathers

The bird has a sedate walk, and often follows farm ploughs picking up leather-jackets and other insects.

Present all year; winter immigrants from Continent.

Young bird has no face-patch, but possesses baggy thigh feathers.

Rooks nest sociably in tall trees, often near farm buildings. Noisy, communal flight displays are common.

SITES GUIDE

Rooks form large feeding flocks in winter, congregating with visitors from continental Europe on open inland or coastal sites.

This bird is widespread, and may be seen at the majority of sites within the range indicated by the map on this page.

Rook *Corvus frugilegus*

Before the leaves are out in spring, rooks congregate in breeding colonies high up in tall trees, their nests standing out against the network of bare branches. This habit of breeding early in conspicuous 'rookeries' makes counting the species relatively easy. The British rook population has fallen recently, possibly because of the ploughing-up of permanent pasture in favour of temporary crops of grass and clover, where the soil does not harbour so many of the bird's favourite insect foods – leather-jackets and wireworms.

Even so, some rookeries may number several thousand pairs: at Hatton Castle near Aberdeen, more than 6,000 nests have been counted. In 1424 James I of Scotland decreed the extermination of the rooks in his kingdom, because of their practice of feeding on corn; but the damage done by the bird to crops may well be balanced by its liking for insect pests.

The rook's nest is a bulky cup of sticks consolidated with soil and lined with roots, leaves, moss or wool. The female builds the nest with materials brought by her mate. A clutch usually consists of three to five bluish-green eggs, with greenish-brown or blackish-green speckles.

Location	Behaviour	Sketch
Date		
Time		
Weather	Field marks	
Call		

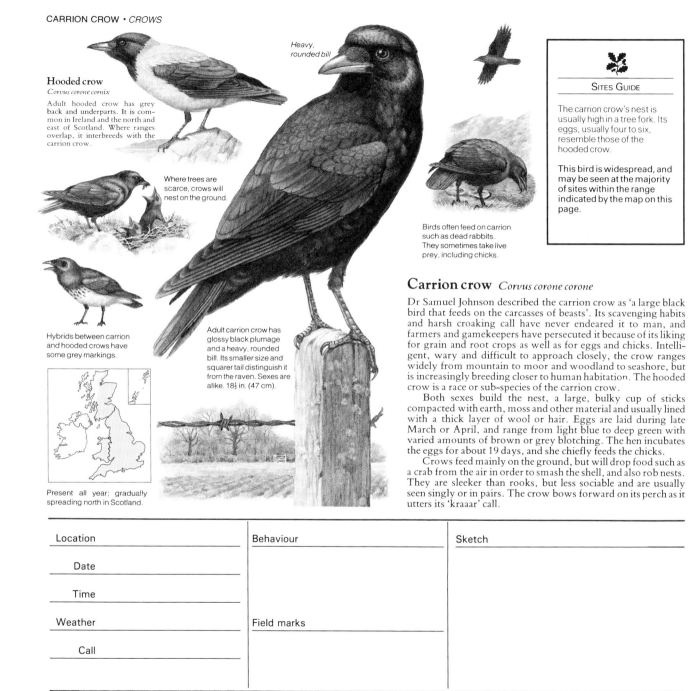

Hooded crow
Corvus corone cornix
Adult hooded crow has grey back and underparts. It is common in Ireland and the north and east of Scotland. Where ranges overlap, it interbreeds with the carrion crow.

Where trees are scarce, crows will nest on the ground.

Hybrids between carrion and hooded crows have some grey markings.

Present all year; gradually spreading north in Scotland.

Adult carrion crow has glossy black plumage and a heavy, rounded bill. Its smaller size and squarer tail distinguish it from the raven. Sexes are alike. 18½ in. (47 cm).

Heavy, rounded bill

Birds often feed on carrion such as dead rabbits. They sometimes take live prey, including chicks.

SITES GUIDE

The carrion crow's nest is usually high in a tree fork. Its eggs, usually four to six, resemble those of the hooded crow.

This bird is widespread, and may be seen at the majority of sites within the range indicated by the map on this page.

Carrion crow *Corvus corone corone*

Dr Samuel Johnson described the carrion crow as 'a large black bird that feeds on the carcasses of beasts'. Its scavenging habits and harsh croaking call have never endeared it to man, and farmers and gamekeepers have persecuted it because of its liking for grain and root crops as well as for eggs and chicks. Intelligent, wary and difficult to approach closely, the crow ranges widely from mountain to moor and woodland to seashore, but is increasingly breeding closer to human habitation. The hooded crow is a race or sub-species of the carrion crow.

Both sexes build the nest, a large, bulky cup of sticks compacted with earth, moss and other material and usually lined with a thick layer of wool or hair. Eggs are laid during late March or April, and range from light blue to deep green with varied amounts of brown or grey blotching. The hen incubates the eggs for about 19 days, and she chiefly feeds the chicks.

Crows feed mainly on the ground, but will drop food such as a crab from the air in order to smash the shell, and also rob nests. They are sleeker than rooks, but less sociable and are usually seen singly or in pairs. The crow bows forward on its perch as it utters its 'kraaar' call.

Location	Behaviour	Sketch
Date		
Time		
Weather	Field marks	
Call		

Waxwings fly swiftly and directly, gliding at intervals. The trilling call-note in flight is distinctive.

Crest

Waxwings are usually very tame, and it is possible to get close enough to identify them.

Bright wings

The bird derives its name from the unusual waxy-looking red tips to its upper flight feathers.

The waxwing is the only buff-brown bird with a crest seen perching during autumn and winter months. Adults of both sexes have a black throat, brightly coloured wings and a yellow tail tip. 7 in. (18 cm).

Nov.–Mar. visitor; numerous only in occasional years.

Garden ponds, woodland pools or roadside puddles provide watering places for thirsty birds.

SITES GUIDE

Waxwings are commonly seen feeding on the year's berry crop. Those that visit Britain are believed to breed in Finland.

The species may be seen at sites numbers: 28, 51.

Waxwing *Bombycilla garrulus*

The waxwing derives its name from the blobs which look like red sealing wax at the tips of some of its secondary flight feathers. It does not breed in Britain, but every few years it erupts in large numbers and turns up in areas well away from its Arctic and sub-Arctic breeding grounds. The reason is not known, but may be connected with the availability of the rowan berry, one of the waxwing's favourite foods in northern latitudes. These invasions are erratic, but a 'waxwing winter' was recorded in Britain as early as 1679–80. The biggest invasion of all was in 1965–6, when more than 11,000 waxwings were recorded in this country.

Waxwings are very gregarious birds, flocking together in small parties to feed on the berries of shrubs such as dog rose, juniper, guelder rose, holly and hawthorn, as well as rowan. Flocks may invade city parks and gardens in search of berries when they become scarce in the countryside.

In the breeding season the waxwings chatter loudly, which led to the bird at one time being known as the 'Bohemian chatterer'. Outside the breeding season, however, it is generally rather a silent bird, occasionally uttering a faint trill.

Location	Behaviour	Sketch
Date		
Time		
Weather	Field marks	
Call		

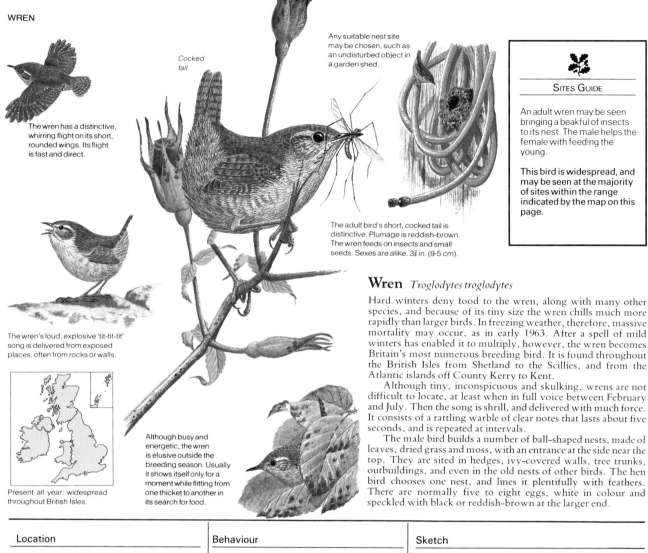

The wren has a distinctive, whirring flight on its short, rounded wings. Its flight is fast and direct.

Cocked tail

Any suitable nest site may be chosen, such as an undisturbed object in a garden shed.

The adult bird's short, cocked tail is distinctive. Plumage is reddish-brown. The wren feeds on insects and small seeds. Sexes are alike. 3¾ in. (9·5 cm).

The wren's loud, explosive 'tit-tit-tit' song is delivered from exposed places, often from rocks or walls.

Present all year; widespread throughout British Isles.

Although busy and energetic, the wren is elusive outside the breeding season. Usually it shows itself only for a moment while flitting from one thicket to another in its search for food.

Wren *Troglodytes troglodytes*

Hard winters deny food to the wren, along with many other species, and because of its tiny size the wren chills much more rapidly than larger birds. In freezing weather, therefore, massive mortality may occur, as in early 1963. After a spell of mild winters has enabled it to multiply, however, the wren becomes Britain's most numerous breeding bird. It is found throughout the British Isles from Shetland to the Scillies, and from the Atlantic islands off County Kerry to Kent.

Although tiny, inconspicuous and skulking, wrens are not difficult to locate, at least when in full voice between February and July. Then the song is shrill, and delivered with much force. It consists of a rattling warble of clear notes that lasts about five seconds, and is repeated at intervals.

The male bird builds a number of ball-shaped nests, made of leaves, dried grass and moss, with an entrance at the side near the top. They are sited in hedges, ivy-covered walls, tree trunks, outbuildings, and even in the old nests of other birds. The hen bird chooses one nest, and lines it plentifully with feathers. There are normally five to eight eggs, white in colour and speckled with black or reddish-brown at the larger end.

Location	Behaviour	Sketch
Date		
Time		
Weather	Field marks	
Call		

Singly or in pairs, dunnocks hop or shuffle across flower-beds searching for insects. On the ground they often flutter their wings.

Dunnocks often rear a young cuckoo from an egg laid in their nest.

Present all year; in Shetlands only passage migrant.

Thin bill

Grey head

The adult is distinguished from other small, brown birds by its grey head and underparts, streaked flanks and thin bill. Sexes alike. 5¾ in. (14·5 cm).

Juvenile birds are spotted, and resemble young robins.

The dunnock's song resembles that of the wren, but lacks the wren's note of aggression.

Dunnock *Prunella modularis*

For many years the dunnock has been called the hedge sparrow, yet it is not related to the sparrow at all. It is a song-bird belonging to the accentor family, many of which live in high mountainous regions. It is widespread throughout Britain in gardens, spinneys, open woodland and wherever there are bushes, shrubs and low scrubby vegetation. It can also be found in open coastal and moorland areas if there is low scrub cover.

The nest, which is built by both birds, is a substantial cup of fine twigs, plant stems, leaves, rootlets and moss, neatly lined with hair, wool or feathers. From three to six, but usually four or five, bright blue eggs are laid. They are incubated for 12–13 days by the female, which leaves the nest frequently to feed. The newly hatched chicks have long black down on their heads and backs. They are fed by both parents, and when begging for food their wide-open beaks reveal bright orange inside the mouth and two black spots on the tongue.

After 12 days the fledglings leave the nest, although they are not very good at flying by then. Two or even three broods may be raised each year. The song is a high-pitched warbling refrain, lasting four or five seconds and repeated at intervals.

Location	Behaviour	Sketch
Date		
Time		
Weather	Field marks	
Call		

The bird is usually seen only briefly in flight as it flits from one bush or tussock to another.

The bird's streaked upper parts and rounded tail are clearly visible at close quarters.

Apr.–Sept. visitor; wide but thin distribution.

Buff underparts

Long tail

Adult bird is brown with whitish-buff underparts and a long tail. A distinctive trilling song sometimes reveals the elusive bird's presence. Sexes are alike. 5 in. (12·5 cm).

The bird's long middle toe enables it to grasp two stems at once when moving among tangled vegetation.

When disturbed, the bird usually creeps away through the grass rather than taking wing.

Grasshopper warbler *Locustella naevia*

A watcher could be forgiven for thinking that the high-pitched whirr that comes from an expanse of tangled grass, bushes and brambles is being produced by some tiny machine. In fact the source of the sound is probably the grasshopper warbler, so named because its song resembles the sound made by some grasshoppers. An attempt to catch sight of the songster, however, is likely to be defeated by its 'voice-throwing' as it turns its head from side to side, and by its shy skulking habits.

The species arrives from winter quarters in north and west Africa between late April and the third week of May. The concealed, cup-shaped nest, approached from one way only, contains usually six creamy eggs, each so thickly speckled with fine purplish-brown spots as to appear dark. Male and female both incubate the eggs, which hatch after two weeks. Nestlings spend 10–12 days in the nest, fed by both parents.

Appetising morsels for grasshopper warblers are small insects and beetles, or spiders and woodlice. The nestlings also receive such succulent items as green caterpillars and aphids. By early August some birds will be flying south again, and by the end of September nearly all will have gone.

Location	Behaviour	Sketch
Date		
Time		
Weather	Field marks	
Call		

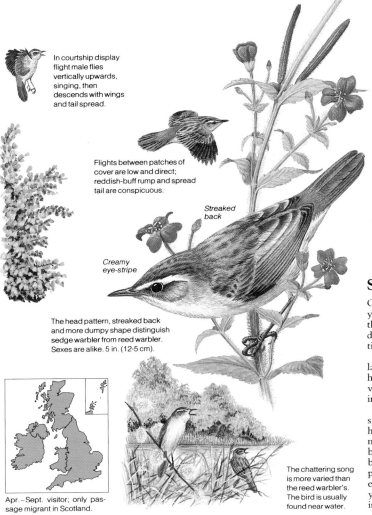

In courtship display flight male flies vertically upwards, singing, then descends with wings and tail spread.

Flights between patches of cover are low and direct; reddish-buff rump and spread tail are conspicuous.

Streaked back

Creamy eye-stripe

The head pattern, streaked back and more dumpy shape distinguish sedge warbler from reed warbler. Sexes are alike. 5 in. (12·5 cm).

Apr.–Sept. visitor; only passage migrant in Scotland.

The chattering song is more varied than the reed warbler's. The bird is usually found near water.

The bird spends much time skulking in cover to hunt for insects.

SITES GUIDE

The sedge warbler's nest is usually built near the ground in dense vegetation.

The species may be seen at sites numbers: 4, 10, 13-15, 25, 27, 35, 41, 42, 45, 49, 52.

Sedge warbler *Acrocephalus schoenobaenus*

One of many species that have benefited from the increase in young forestry plantations is the sedge warbler. It adapts well to their dense, rank vegetation, although it is traditionally a bird of damper areas such as osiers or reed-beds; it also occurs sometimes in standing crops.

Its attractive song, occasionally performed at night, is similar to the reed warbler's but more varied – a continuous and hurried series of notes, some chattering, some musical, each variant usually being repeated several times. Its own song is interspersed with accurate mimicry of other birds' songs.

Although more widespread than the reed warbler, this elusive bird is hard to spot, as it hides itself in low vegetation, hunting insects; and when it does emerge it darts straight to the next patch of cover. But its identity will be revealed by even a brief glimpse. Its colour is creamier than the reed warbler's, with bold streaks of darker colour on the back and wings and a prominent, creamy stripe above each eye. Usually five or six eggs are laid in a nest hidden low down in dense vegetation. The young, which hatch after about two weeks, are fed on small insects such as crane-flies, midges, beetles and dragonflies.

Location	Behaviour	Sketch
Date		
Time		
Weather	Field marks	
Call		

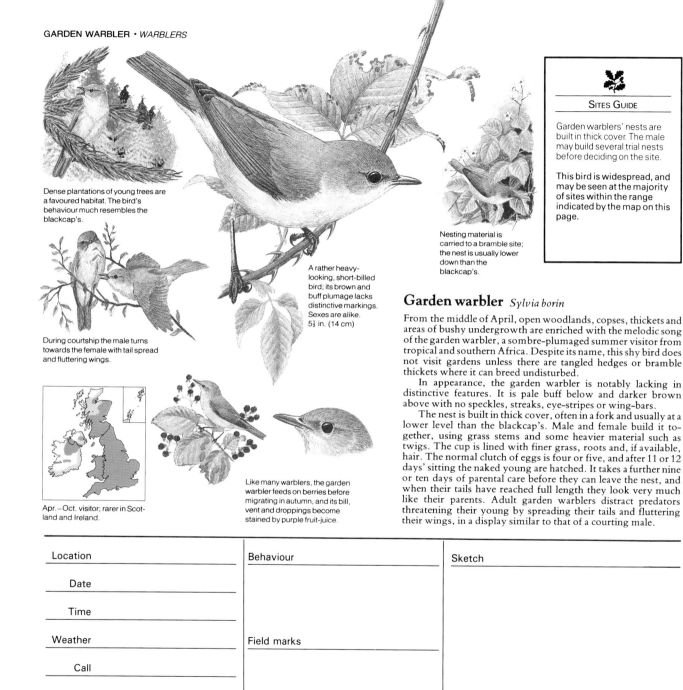

Dense plantations of young trees are a favoured habitat. The bird's behaviour much resembles the blackcap's.

During courtship the male turns towards the female with tail spread and fluttering wings.

A rather heavy-looking, short-billed bird; its brown and buff plumage lacks distinctive markings. Sexes are alike. 5½ in. (14 cm)

Apr.–Oct. visitor; rarer in Scotland and Ireland.

Like many warblers, the garden warbler feeds on berries before migrating in autumn, and its bill, vent and droppings become stained by purple fruit-juice.

SITES GUIDE

Garden warblers' nests are built in thick cover. The male may build several trial nests before deciding on the site.

This bird is widespread, and may be seen at the majority of sites within the range indicated by the map on this page.

Nesting material is carried to a bramble site; the nest is usually lower down than the blackcap's.

Garden warbler *Sylvia borin*

From the middle of April, open woodlands, copses, thickets and areas of bushy undergrowth are enriched with the melodic song of the garden warbler, a sombre-plumaged summer visitor from tropical and southern Africa. Despite its name, this shy bird does not visit gardens unless there are tangled hedges or bramble thickets where it can breed undisturbed.

In appearance, the garden warbler is notably lacking in distinctive features. It is pale buff below and darker brown above with no speckles, streaks, eye-stripes or wing-bars.

The nest is built in thick cover, often in a fork and usually at a lower level than the blackcap's. Male and female build it together, using grass stems and some heavier material such as twigs. The cup is lined with finer grass, roots and, if available, hair. The normal clutch of eggs is four or five, and after 11 or 12 days' sitting the naked young are hatched. It takes a further nine or ten days of parental care before they can leave the nest, and when their tails have reached full length they look very much like their parents. Adult garden warblers distract predators threatening their young by spreading their tails and fluttering their wings, in a display similar to that of a courting male.

Location	Behaviour	Sketch
Date		
Time		
Weather	Field marks	
Call		

Some blackcaps winter in Britain and may visit gardens for scraps in the snow.

Male: black cap

Female: brown cap

A male with nest material. Males build several frail 'cock's nests' in addition to the main nest built by both sexes.

Apr.–Oct. visitor; some winter, mainly in south-west.

The striking black cap distinguishes the male from all other warblers. The female's brown cap is less striking. 5½ in. (14 cm).

A female feeds her chicks. Young birds all have brown caps.

Courting males assume extraordinary postures. Cap feathers are raised, wings drooped and tails spread.

SITES GUIDE

The nest of the blackcap is usually sited in a thick bush, just concealed from predators by the outer leaves.

This bird is widespread, and may be seen at the majority of sites within the range indicated by the map on this page.

Blackcap *Sylvia atricapilla*

Unless he can spot the characteristic jet-black crown, a bird-watcher may have difficulty in distinguishing the blackcap from the garden warbler. Both are shy, live in thick cover and greet the intruder with a loud, scolding 'tacc-tacc' like two stones struck together. The blackcap's rich song, however, most often heard from March to July, is usually more variable in pitch, and delivered in shorter bursts.

The blackcap nests in woods, tall hedgerows and gardens with plenty of brambles and briers. It can most typically be seen picking its way through the branches and stems, searching for insect food such as flies and caterpillars between bouts of singing.

The nests, hidden in bushes or undergrowth, are neatly built but flimsy cups of dry grass and roots, lined with finer strands of grass, roots and hair. The four to six eggs are incubated by both parents for 10–14 days. Most blackcaps leave for tropical Africa in August or September; unlike garden warblers, blackcaps complete their moult before migrating. In recent years a few blackcaps have taken to braving the English winter, visiting bird-tables for food.

Location	Behaviour	Sketch
Date		
Time		
Weather	Field marks	
Call		

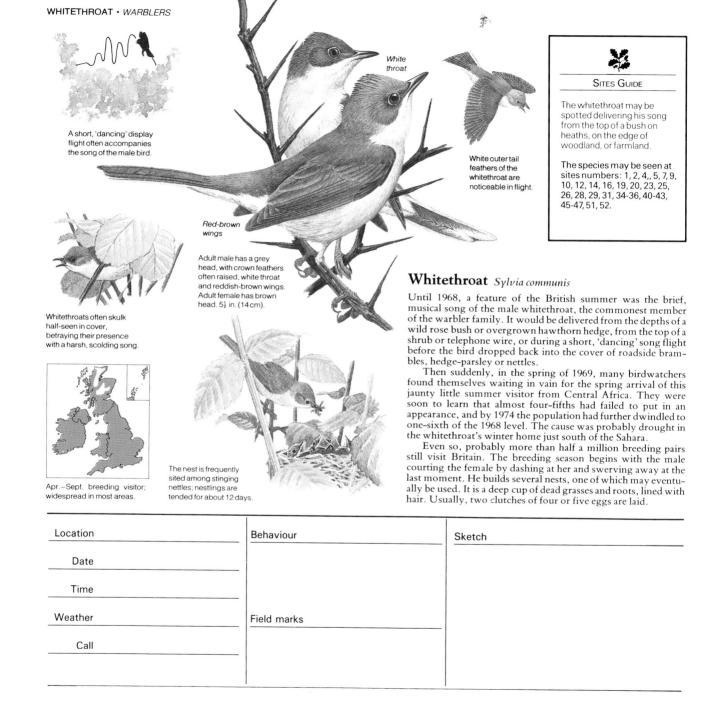

A short, 'dancing' display flight often accompanies the song of the male bird.

White throat

White outer tail feathers of the whitethroat are noticeable in flight.

Red-brown wings

Whitethroats often skulk half-seen in cover, betraying their presence with a harsh, scolding song.

Adult male has a grey head, with crown feathers often raised, white throat and reddish-brown wings. Adult female has brown head. 5½ in. (14 cm).

Apr.–Sept. breeding visitor; widespread in most areas.

The nest is frequently sited among stinging nettles; nestlings are tended for about 12 days.

SITES GUIDE

The whitethroat may be spotted delivering his song from the top of a bush on heaths, on the edge of woodland, or farmland.

The species may be seen at sites numbers: 1, 2, 4,, 5, 7, 9, 10, 12, 14, 16, 19, 20, 23, 25, 26, 28, 29, 31, 34-36, 40-43, 45-47, 51, 52.

Whitethroat *Sylvia communis*

Until 1968, a feature of the British summer was the brief, musical song of the male whitethroat, the commonest member of the warbler family. It would be delivered from the depths of a wild rose bush or overgrown hawthorn hedge, from the top of a shrub or telephone wire, or during a short, 'dancing' song flight before the bird dropped back into the cover of roadside brambles, hedge–parsley or nettles.

Then suddenly, in the spring of 1969, many birdwatchers found themselves waiting in vain for the spring arrival of this jaunty little summer visitor from Central Africa. They were soon to learn that almost four-fifths had failed to put in an appearance, and by 1974 the population had further dwindled to one-sixth of the 1968 level. The cause was probably drought in the whitethroat's winter home just south of the Sahara.

Even so, probably more than half a million breeding pairs still visit Britain. The breeding season begins with the male courting the female by dashing at her and swerving away at the last moment. He builds several nests, one of which may eventually be used. It is a deep cup of dead grasses and roots, lined with hair. Usually, two clutches of four or five eggs are laid.

Location	Behaviour	Sketch
Date		
Time		
Weather	Field marks	
Call		

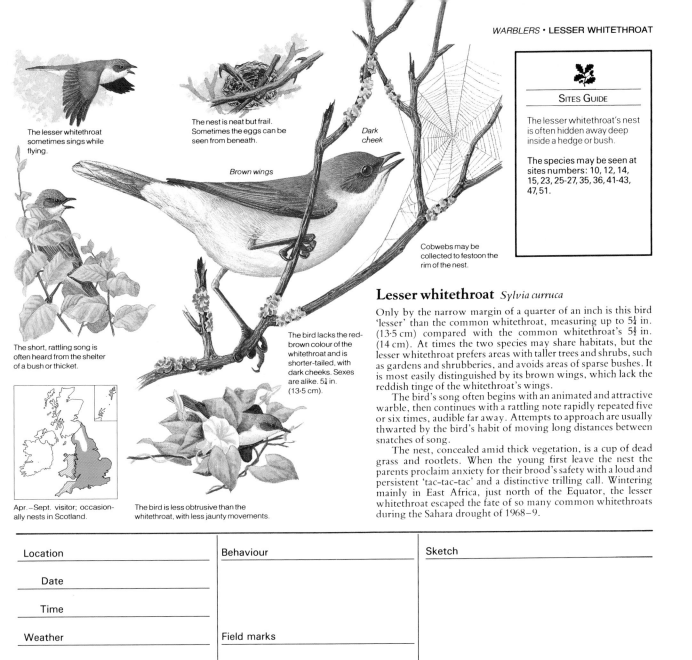

The lesser whitethroat sometimes sings while flying.

The nest is neat but frail. Sometimes the eggs can be seen from beneath.

Dark cheek

Brown wings

Cobwebs may be collected to festoon the rim of the nest.

The short, rattling song is often heard from the shelter of a bush or thicket.

The bird lacks the red-brown colour of the whitethroat and is shorter-tailed, with dark cheeks. Sexes are alike. 5¼ in. (13·5 cm).

Apr.–Sept. visitor; occasionally nests in Scotland.

The bird is less obtrusive than the whitethroat, with less jaunty movements.

Lesser whitethroat *Sylvia curruca*

Only by the narrow margin of a quarter of an inch is this bird 'lesser' than the common whitethroat, measuring up to 5¼ in. (13·5 cm) compared with the common whitethroat's 5¼ in. (14 cm). At times the two species may share habitats, but the lesser whitethroat prefers areas with taller trees and shrubs, such as gardens and shrubberies, and avoids areas of sparse bushes. It is most easily distinguished by its brown wings, which lack the reddish tinge of the whitethroat's wings.

The bird's song often begins with an animated and attractive warble, then continues with a rattling note rapidly repeated five or six times, audible far away. Attempts to approach are usually thwarted by the bird's habit of moving long distances between snatches of song.

The nest, concealed amid thick vegetation, is a cup of dead grass and rootlets. When the young first leave the nest the parents proclaim anxiety for their brood's safety with a loud and persistent 'tac-tac-tac' and a distinctive trilling call. Wintering mainly in East Africa, just north of the Equator, the lesser whitethroat escaped the fate of so many common whitethroats during the Sahara drought of 1968–9.

Location	Behaviour	Sketch
Date		
Time		
Weather	Field marks	
Call		

Male in courting display rears up with its tail fanned out and makes its wings quiver.

Olive above

Yellowish below

Flights are usually short, from one tree to another near by.

Feeding bird darts restlessly about among foliage, seeking its insect prey.

Pale legs

Bird looks plumper than chiffchaff; underparts yellower, legs paler. Sexes alike; 4½ in. (12 cm).

Apr. – Sept. visitor, breeding in wood and shrubland.

Young birds have much stronger yellow tinge than adult.

SITES GUIDE

The willow warbler's domed, feather-lined nest of moss and grass is usually built on the ground.

This bird is widespread, and may be seen at the majority of sites within the range indicated by the map on this page.

Willow warbler *Phylloscopus trochilus*

Filling the summer countryside with its sweetly wistful song, the willow warbler is the most widely distributed of all the birds that visit Britain in the breeding season. Almost any area of woodland or shrubs is suitable – the bird has no special preference for willow – as long as the foliage does not form a closed canopy. The total British Isles population is probably more than three million pairs.

When its cadence of soft, liquid notes can no longer be heard, early in autumn, this determined little bird has started its annual 2,500 mile (4,000 km) journey to tropical and southern Africa. The wear and tear of this taxing migration may account for the willow warbler's curious distinction among British birds: it moults completely, replacing all its plumage, twice a year. Even its close relative the chiffchaff moults only once. Nevertheless the willow warbler is able to produce two broods in most breeding seasons, while the chiffchaff manages only one.

The domed nest with its side opening usually contains six eggs, white with pinkish or reddish-brown speckles. The hen alone incubates them, taking about 13 days, but the male helps in feeding the chicks during the 13 days they spend in the nest.

Location	Behaviour	Sketch
Date		
Time		
Weather	Field marks	
Call		

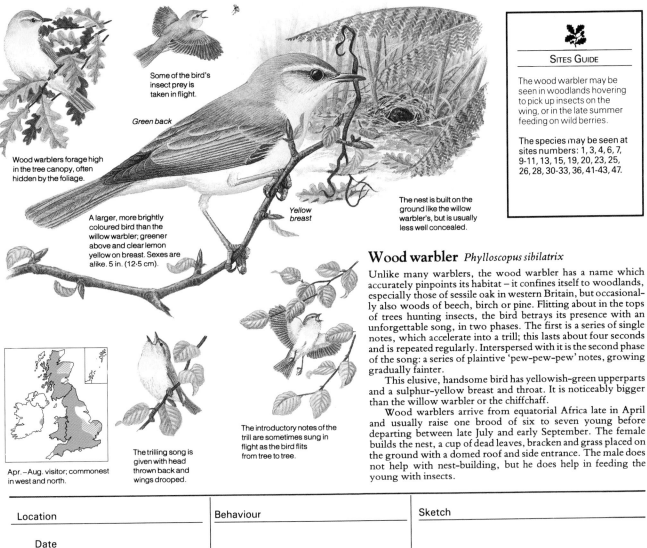

Some of the bird's insect prey is taken in flight.

Green back

Wood warblers forage high in the tree canopy, often hidden by the foliage.

A larger, more brightly coloured bird than the willow warbler; greener above and clear lemon yellow on breast. Sexes are alike. 5 in. (12·5 cm).

Yellow breast

The nest is built on the ground like the willow warbler's, but is usually less well concealed.

Apr.–Aug. visitor; commonest in west and north.

The trilling song is given with head thrown back and wings drooped.

The introductory notes of the trill are sometimes sung in flight as the bird flits from tree to tree.

SITES GUIDE

The wood warbler may be seen in woodlands hovering to pick up insects on the wing, or in the late summer feeding on wild berries.

The species may be seen at sites numbers: 1, 3, 4, 6, 7, 9-11, 13, 15, 19, 20, 23, 25, 26, 28, 30-33, 36, 41-43, 47.

Wood warbler *Phylloscopus sibilatrix*

Unlike many warblers, the wood warbler has a name which accurately pinpoints its habitat – it confines itself to woodlands, especially those of sessile oak in western Britain, but occasionally also woods of beech, birch or pine. Flitting about in the tops of trees hunting insects, the bird betrays its presence with an unforgettable song, in two phases. The first is a series of single notes, which accelerate into a trill; this lasts about four seconds and is repeated regularly. Interspersed with it is the second phase of the song: a series of plaintive 'pew-pew-pew' notes, growing gradually fainter.

This elusive, handsome bird has yellowish-green upperparts and a sulphur-yellow breast and throat. It is noticeably bigger than the willow warbler or the chiffchaff.

Wood warblers arrive from equatorial Africa late in April and usually raise one brood of six to seven young before departing between late July and early September. The female builds the nest, a cup of dead leaves, bracken and grass placed on the ground with a domed roof and side entrance. The male does not help with nest-building, but he does help in feeding the young with insects.

Location	Behaviour	Sketch
Date		
Time		
Weather	Field marks	
Call		

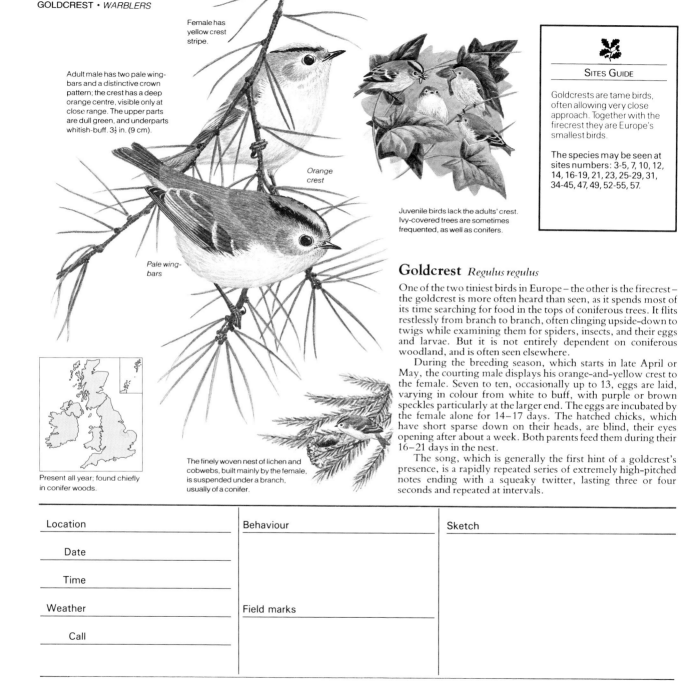

Female has yellow crest stripe.

Adult male has two pale wing-bars and a distinctive crown pattern; the crest has a deep orange centre, visible only at close range. The upper parts are dull green, and underparts whitish-buff. 3½ in. (9 cm).

Orange crest

Pale wing-bars

Juvenile birds lack the adults' crest. Ivy-covered trees are sometimes frequented, as well as conifers.

Present all year; found chiefly in conifer woods.

The finely woven nest of lichen and cobwebs, built mainly by the female, is suspended under a branch, usually of a conifer.

Goldcrest *Regulus regulus*

One of the two tiniest birds in Europe – the other is the firecrest – the goldcrest is more often heard than seen, as it spends most of its time searching for food in the tops of coniferous trees. It flits restlessly from branch to branch, often clinging upside-down to twigs while examining them for spiders, insects, and their eggs and larvae. But it is not entirely dependent on coniferous woodland, and is often seen elsewhere.

During the breeding season, which starts in late April or May, the courting male displays his orange-and-yellow crest to the female. Seven to ten, occasionally up to 13, eggs are laid, varying in colour from white to buff, with purple or brown speckles particularly at the larger end. The eggs are incubated by the female alone for 14–17 days. The hatched chicks, which have short sparse down on their heads, are blind, their eyes opening after about a week. Both parents feed them during their 16–21 days in the nest.

The song, which is generally the first hint of a goldcrest's presence, is a rapidly repeated series of extremely high-pitched notes ending with a squeaky twitter, lasting three or four seconds and repeated at intervals.

Location	Behaviour	Sketch
Date		
Time		
Weather	Field marks	
Call		

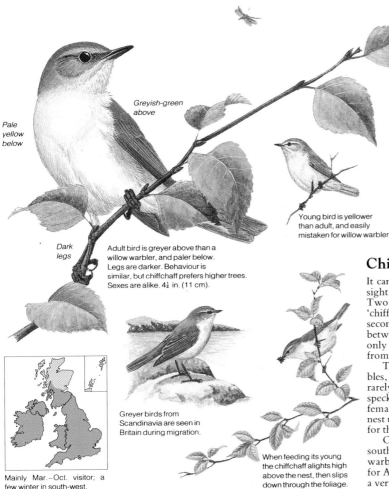

Greyish-green above

Pale yellow below

Dark legs

Adult bird is greyer above than a willow warbler, and paler below. Legs are darker. Behaviour is similar, but chiffchaff prefers higher trees. Sexes are alike. 4¼ in. (11 cm).

Young bird is yellower than adult, and easily mistaken for willow warbler.

Courting male 'floats' down to female on spread wings.

Greyer birds from Scandinavia are seen in Britain during migration.

When feeding its young the chiffchaff alights high above the nest, then slips down through the foliage.

Mainly Mar.–Oct. visitor; a few winter in south-west.

Chiffchaff *Phylloscopus collybita*

It can be difficult to tell a chiffchaff from a willow warbler by sight alone, but the chiffchaff's far-carrying song gives it away. Two notes are uttered in random order: one a high-pitched 'chiff' or 'tsip', the other a lower 'chaff' or 'tsap'. After 15 seconds or so the bird seems to fall silent, but in the intervals between songs it often gives a soft, chirring call that is audible only at close range. Unlike the willow warbler, it likes to sing from high in a tree.

The female chiffchaff hides its ball-shaped nest among brambles, nettles or other dense vegetation, near the ground but rarely on it. The six or seven white eggs have purplish-brown speckles. They are incubated for less than a fortnight by the female, which is sometimes fed by its mate but usually leaves the nest unattended when it is hungry. The male helps to bring food for the chicks during the two weeks they stay in the nest.

One of the hardier migratory warblers, the chiffchaff flies south for the winter two or three weeks later than the willow warbler, and usually returns a fortnight or so earlier. Most head for Africa, although some go only as far as southern Europe and a very few winter in south-west England.

Location	Behaviour	Sketch
Date		
Time		
Weather	Field marks	
Call		

Juvenile lacks crest, but is identifiable by its eye-stripe.

The crest is raised and spread when the courting male is displaying.

Orange crest

Eye-stripe

SITES GUIDE

The firecrest is an agile bird, and can often be seen clinging to the underside of twigs as it searches for insects.

The species may be seen at sites numbers: 10, 15, 27, 45.

In winter, firecrests and goldcrests may be seen with groups of tits.

Adult bird is distinguished from goldcrest by its black-and-white eye-stripe, and a bronze tinge on the sides of the neck is visible at close quarters. Plumage in general is brighter than that of the goldcrest. Sexes are alike. 3½ in. (9 cm).

Passage migrant; some breed or winter in Britain.

Firecrest *Regulus ignicapillus*

Although very similar to the goldcrest, the firecrest can be identified chiefly by its black-and-white eye-stripes. The song also helps to distinguish the bird; it is similar in tone and pitch to the goldcrest's, but is simpler and lacks the squeaky twitter at the end. The call is a short 'zit-zit', rather harsher than the goldcrest's 'see-see'.

There are other slight differences between the two birds and their behaviour. The firecrest's nest tends to be slightly smaller and more compact, the breeding season begins a little later, and the eggs tend to be pink rather than buff. Despite these differences, however, there is often considerable rivalry between the two species.

Norway spruce forests are the bird's favourite habitat in England, but it can also be found in a variety of other conifer and deciduous woods. The firecrest is chiefly a passage migrant, seen mainly in southern England in autumn and winter, but it has bred in Britain. This fact first became evident in 1962, when fully fledged young were seen. There have been many other instances of likely breeding in Britain, though the number of sightings has dropped considerably in recent years.

Location	Behaviour	Sketch
Date		
Time		
Weather	Field marks	
Call		

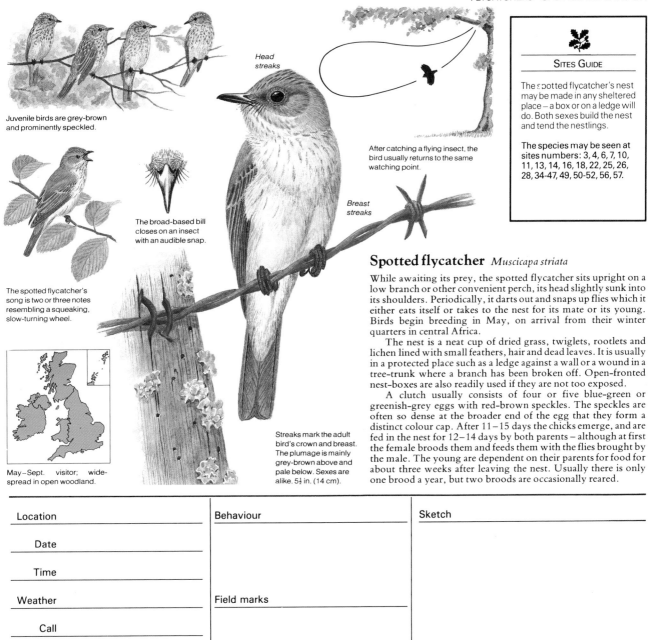

Juvenile birds are grey-brown and prominently speckled.

The spotted flycatcher's song is two or three notes resembling a squeaking, slow-turning wheel.

The broad-based bill closes on an insect with an audible snap.

Head streaks

After catching a flying insect, the bird usually returns to the same watching point.

Breast streaks

May–Sept. visitor; widespread in open woodland.

Streaks mark the adult bird's crown and breast. The plumage is mainly grey-brown above and pale below. Sexes are alike. 5½ in. (14 cm).

SITES GUIDE

The spotted flycatcher's nest may be made in any sheltered place – a box or on a ledge will do. Both sexes build the nest and tend the nestlings.

The species may be seen at sites numbers: 3, 4, 6, 7, 10, 11, 13, 14, 16, 18, 22, 25, 26, 28, 34-47, 49, 50-52, 56, 57.

Spotted flycatcher *Muscicapa striata*

While awaiting its prey, the spotted flycatcher sits upright on a low branch or other convenient perch, its head slightly sunk into its shoulders. Periodically, it darts out and snaps up flies which it either eats itself or takes to the nest for its mate or its young. Birds begin breeding in May, on arrival from their winter quarters in central Africa.

The nest is a neat cup of dried grass, twiglets, rootlets and lichen lined with small feathers, hair and dead leaves. It is usually in a protected place such as a ledge against a wall or a wound in a tree-trunk where a branch has been broken off. Open-fronted nest-boxes are also readily used if they are not too exposed.

A clutch usually consists of four or five blue-green or greenish-grey eggs with red-brown speckles. The speckles are often so dense at the broader end of the egg that they form a distinct colour cap. After 11–15 days the chicks emerge, and are fed in the nest for 12–14 days by both parents – although at first the female broods them and feeds them with the flies brought by the male. The young are dependent on their parents for food for about three weeks after leaving the nest. Usually there is only one brood a year, but two broods are occasionally reared.

Location	Behaviour	Sketch
Date		
Time		
Weather	Field marks	
Call		

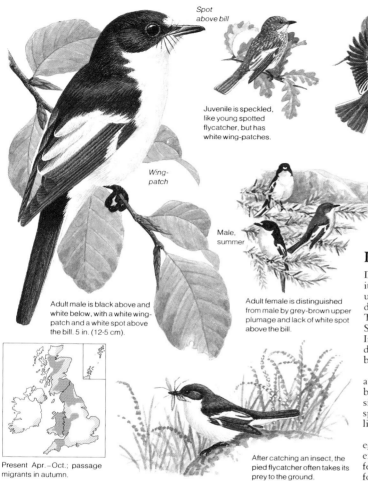

Spot above bill

Juvenile is speckled, like young spotted flycatcher, but has white wing-patches.

Pied flycatchers glean prey such as caterpillars from tree foliage, as well as catching insects in flight.

Wing-patch

Male, summer

Female, summer

Adult male is black above and white below, with a white wing-patch and a white spot above the bill. 5 in. (12·5 cm).

Adult female is distinguished from male by grey-brown upper plumage and lack of white spot above the bill.

Present Apr.–Oct.; passage migrants in autumn.

After catching an insect, the pied flycatcher often takes its prey to the ground.

Sites Guide

The pied flycatcher is always on the lookout for insects; but after darting out in attack, seldom returns to the same perch.

The species may be seen at sites numbers: 3, 7, 10, 11, 13, 16, 25, 28, 31-33, 36, 45, 48, 52-55.

Pied flycatcher *Ficedula hypoleuca*

During the last 40 years or so, the pied flycatcher has extended its breeding range from Wales to the valleys and foothills of upland England. This increase may have been assisted by the deliberate provision of nest-boxes by bird lovers in some areas. The bird is also found to a lesser extent in the Pennines, southern Scotland and the Scottish Highlands; but it is not seen at all in Ireland. Unlike the spotted flycatcher, male and female have different breeding plumage, although in autumn the male's black upper parts dull to the female's grey-brown colour.

The pied flycatcher needs a plentiful supply of caterpillars and other insects on which to feed. Tree-stumps and dead branches provide ideal song posts and holes for nesting. The nest site is chosen by the male when he arrives from Africa in the spring. The female follows a little later and builds the nest. She lines it with animal hair, wool and feathers.

The single, annual clutch usually consists of four to seven eggs. They are pale blue, and very occasionally have a few extremely fine, reddish-brown speckles. The male feeds the female while she is incubating the eggs, which takes just under a fortnight. The young can fly after about two weeks.

Location	Behaviour	Sketch
Date		
Time		
Weather	Field marks	
Call		

Adult female is brown above and paler below; she has a rusty tail, like the male.

Adult female can be distinguished from the nightingale by the dark centre of the tail, which is not rounded.

Juvenile bird is brown and speckled.

Grey back

Adult male redstart has a rust-coloured tail (or 'start'), reddish belly, grey back, black throat and conspicuous white blaze on forehead. 5½ in. (14 cm).

Rusty tail

Apr.–Sept. visitor, which occasionally breeds in Ireland.

During migration many birds may be found resting and feeding along the shore line.

Redstart *Phoenicurus phoenicurus*

With its richly contrasting colours and distinctive markings, the redstart is one of Britain's handsomest small birds. Its most noticeable feature is its bright russet tail, and to this it owes its name: *steort* is Anglo-Saxon for 'tail'. The constantly flickering tail plays an important part in the bird's courtship ritual, during which the male splays its tail feathers to reveal the brilliant rust-coloured splash.

The bird commonly breeds in deciduous woodland, parkland, gardens or mature orchards; it also breeds in more open country if there are suitable nest sites, such as stone walls and tree holes. Nests, built by the female, are loosely constructed cups of dead grass, rootlets, moss and bark fragments, lined with finer materials such as hair and feathers. The usual clutch consists of five to seven eggs, which are incubated for about two weeks by the female alone. When the chicks are hatched the male helps to feed them for the 12–16 days they remain in the nest.

The alarm note of the redstart is an anxious 'wee-ticc-ticc'; its song is a brief but melodious warble terminating in a jingling rattle. Most of the breeding population depart in the autumn for winter quarters in tropical Africa.

Location	Behaviour	Sketch
Date		
Time		
Weather	Field marks	
Call		

Adult male is sooty black, with a white wing-patch and rust-coloured tail. 5¼ in. (14 cm).

White patch

Rusty tail

Wing-patches show prominently when the bird hovers to catch its insect prey.

Adult female is less black than the male, and lacks the white wing-patch.

The juvenile bird has speckled plumage but is otherwise similar to the adult female.

Small numbers breed; a few winter in south.

Migrating birds are often seen on rocky beaches. They can be distinguished from redstarts by darker breasts and greyer upper parts.

Sites Guide

For the black redstart, breeding begins in late April. Nests, in crevices, are usually made of grass, moss and roots, lined with feathers.

The species may be seen at site number: 46.

Black redstart *Phoenicurus ochruros*

Until the Second World War, black redstarts were rare breeding birds in Britain. The rubble and broken walls of bombed sites, however, provided an environment similar to the rock-falls, screes and boulder-strewn hillsides which are the birds' natural habitat on the Continent, and their numbers increased considerably. Now, an average of 30 pairs breed in Britain each year. As bomb damage was repaired after the war, some black redstarts moved to other nesting places, such as factory sites, gasworks and railway yards. Others occupy coastal cliffs.

The nest, normally built by the female alone, is a loose cup of dried grass, moss or rootlets, lined with hair, wool or feathers. It is built on a ledge or in a wall where a brick is missing, or in some other crevice; hollow trees are also sometimes used. The clutch of four to six white eggs is incubated for 12–16 days by the female, and young birds remain in the nest for 16–18 days. Often the female produces two broods, and occasionally three. The male helps with feeding, bringing beakfuls of insects.

The black redstart's song is distinctive: a fairly loud, brief, reedy warble, which can sometimes be heard from rooftops above the din of traffic.

Location	Behaviour	Sketch
Date		
Time		
Weather	Field marks	
Call		

Juvenile bird's tail colouring and paler underparts distinguish it from a young robin.

Chestnut tail is conspicuous on rare glimpse of nightingale in flight.

A chestnut tail is the only eye-catching feature of the adult bird, which is like an oversized robin in build and attitude. Seldom seen, it is usually identified by its song. Sexes are alike. 6½ in. (16·5 cm).

Chestnut tail

A feeding bird may dart out of hiding to find insects.

Apr.–Aug. visitor; rare outside breeding range.

SITES GUIDE

The nightingale nest, of dead leaves lined with grass and hair, is usually hidden in brambles or nettles, on or close to the ground.

The species may be seen at sites numbers: 14, 16, 23, 25, 26, 38, 41, 45-47.

The characteristic tail colour is usually all that is seen as the bird dives for cover.

Nightingale *Luscinia megarhynchos*

Generations of poets have been inspired by the song of the nightingale. Milton, for instance, wrote of the 'nightingale, that on yon bloomy spray Warbl'st at eve, when all the woods are still'. The song, sometimes but not always delivered at dead of night, is remarkable for its tonal richness, variety and volume. It consists of a series of short phrases and single notes, usually repeated, often with increasing volume, some notes having a flute-like quality, others a more piping tone. The song period is short, lasting only from mid to late April until June.

The nightingale is a shy bird, generally to be found in open deciduous woodland where plenty of cover is provided by dense undergrowth of bramble, or by thickets of thorn bushes such as blackthorn. However, because the nightingale feeds largely on ground-living insects such as beetles, any site which has become too overgrown is deserted.

The four or five eggs laid in May are olive-green or olive-brown. Incubation takes about two weeks and is by the female alone. The young are fed for about 12 days by both parents. By the end of July many birds have started their journey back to Africa; and the stragglers have gone by the end of September.

Location	Behaviour	Sketch
Date		
Time		
Weather	Field marks	
Call		

Red breast

The cock robin's pleasant warbling, heard all year except during late-summer moulting, is a reminder of claim to a territory.

Adult bird's red face and breast, with pale grey border, identify it easily. Upper parts and tail are brown and underparts whitish. Sexes are alike. 5½ in. (14 cm).

Present all year; Continental migrants in east and south.

Robins are generally pugnacious, and the male birds are vigorously aggressive in territorial disputes.

Any convenient hole or ledge – even an old container such as a tea-pot – may be chosen as a nesting place.

Although regarded as tame and confident, robins sometimes behave secretively, especially during the late-summer moult.

Robin *Erithacus rubecula*

For generations, the robin has earned its place as Britain's best-loved bird. It is noted for its tameness in town and city gardens, and often searches for food around the feet of gardeners who are turning over the ground. It will even eat meal-worms straight from the hand. Away from habitation, however, in woodland and other areas of countryside, the robin is more wary, and on the Continent it is a shy and retiring bird.

It is extremely possessive of its territory, and guards it fiercely from other robins. The nest is built entirely by the female and,is usually hidden amongst thick ivy on trees or walls, or among roots or undergrowth on banks. Nests are also commonly found inside sheds and other buildings; and sauce-pans, old tins and the like are readily commandeered for nesting.

Breeding begins from late March in the south to June in the north. A clutch usually consists of five to six eggs, which are incubated by the female for 12–15 days. Young birds leave the nest after about two weeks. The male may take over the feeding and care of one brood if a second clutch follows quickly. The robin has a loud, penetrating 'tic–tic' alarm call and a thin, rather sad but sweet warbling song, consisting of short phrases.

Location	Behaviour	Sketch
Date		
Time		
Weather	Field marks	
Call		

Adult male is all black, with orange bill and yellow eye-ring. 10 in. (25 cm).

Orange bill

The plumage of a young bird resembles that of the female, but is more distinctly spotted.

Albino males, with white feathers, are often seen in town gardens.

A blackbird will stand with its head cocked on one side, listening for worms.

Adult female looks all brown at a distance, but has blurred spots on throat and breast.

Young males, still with their first-winter black bill, are often seen feeding on hawthorn berries in winter, together with migrant thrushes such as redwings.

Present all year; continental birds winter in Britain.

Blackbird *Turdus merula*

'I value my garden more for being full of blackbirds than of cherries, and very frankly give them fruit for their songs,' declared the 18th-century essayist Joseph Addison in *The Spectator*. Most people would agree with Addison. For the rich, short, fluty warbling, punctuated by pauses, that the blackbird delivers from any suitable vantage point – tree, rooftop or TV aerial – is a welcome herald of spring. When danger threatens, the blackbird gives a harsh, persistent 'pink-pink-pink-pink' call which is repeated until the peril has passed.

Blackbirds, among the commonest of British birds, eat fruit and berries in season and also feed on worms and insects. In the mating season, the black-plumaged male is conspicuous for its display, which involves much running about with rump feathers raised, tail fanned and wings drooped. Nest-building is left mainly to the female, which makes a solid cup of dried grass, rootlets, twigs and moss, lined with mud and dried grass.

The pale, blue-green, speckled eggs, usually three to five, are laid from March to April; they hatch in about a fortnight. The young leave the nest 14 days or so later, but can only flutter and depend on the parents for food for about another three weeks.

Location	Behaviour	Sketch
Date		
Time		
Weather	Field marks	
Call		

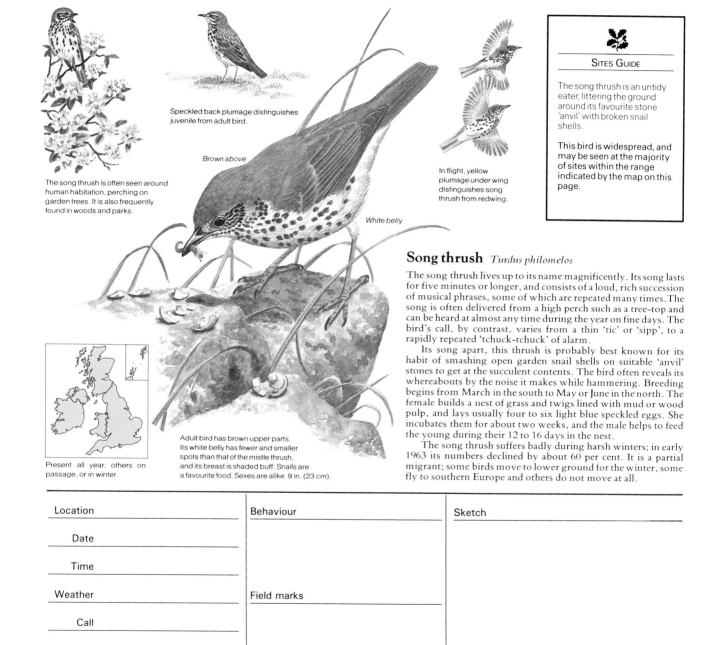

Speckled back plumage distinguishes juvenile from adult bird.

Brown above

The song thrush is often seen around human habitation, perching on garden trees. It is also frequently found in woods and parks.

White belly

In flight, yellow plumage under wing distinguishes song thrush from redwing.

Sites Guide

The song thrush is an untidy eater, littering the ground around its favourite stone 'anvil' with broken snail shells.

This bird is widespread, and may be seen at the majority of sites within the range indicated by the map on this page.

Present all year; others on passage, or in winter.

Adult bird has brown upper parts. Its white belly has fewer and smaller spots than that of the mistle thrush, and its breast is shaded buff. Snails are a favourite food. Sexes are alike. 9 in. (23 cm).

Song thrush *Turdus philomelos*

The song thrush lives up to its name magnificently. Its song lasts for five minutes or longer, and consists of a loud, rich succession of musical phrases, some of which are repeated many times. The song is often delivered from a high perch such as a tree-top and can be heard at almost any time during the year on fine days. The bird's call, by contrast, varies from a thin 'tic' or 'sipp', to a rapidly repeated 'tchuck–tchuck' of alarm.

Its song apart, this thrush is probably best known for its habit of smashing open garden snail shells on suitable 'anvil' stones to get at the succulent contents. The bird often reveals its whereabouts by the noise it makes while hammering. Breeding begins from March in the south to May or June in the north. The female builds a nest of grass and twigs lined with mud or wood pulp, and lays usually four to six light blue speckled eggs. She incubates them for about two weeks, and the male helps to feed the young during their 12 to 16 days in the nest.

The song thrush suffers badly during harsh winters; in early 1963 its numbers declined by about 60 per cent. It is a partial migrant; some birds move to lower ground for the winter, some fly to southern Europe and others do not move at all.

Location	Behaviour	Sketch
Date		
Time		
Weather	Field marks	
Call		

Grey-brown upper parts and bold brown spots on a white breast distinguish the mistle thrush – the largest of the British thrushes – from the song thrush. Sexes are alike. 10½ in. (27 cm).

Grey-brown above

Both wings are closed at regular intervals in flight, which is strong and direct.

Large breast spots

In flight, its white underwing helps to distinguish the bird from other thrushes.

The plumage of juvenile birds is more speckled than adults'.

Present all year. Some birds winter on Continent.

Small family groups often move about together when the breeding season is over.

Sites Guide

The hen mistle thrush builds a bulky, grass-lined nest of twigs, grass, earth and moss, usually in the fork of a high branch.

This bird is widespread, and may be seen at the majority of sites within the range indicated by the map on this page.

Mistle thrush *Turdus viscivorus*

The mistle thrush is also known as the 'storm cock', for it sings through the stormy days of winter as well as the fine days; indeed, its song was often believed to give warning of a coming storm. The song is a prolonged series of short fluty notes of varying pitch and considerable carrying power, sung usually from the topmost swaying twigs of high trees. In flight its call is a short rattling chatter, which becomes louder and more prolonged when the bird is alarmed.

Nest-building, by the female alone, takes place from February onwards. Three to five eggs, varying in colour from cream to turquoise, with purplish-brown spots, are usually laid. These are incubated by the female for 12–15 days. The male helps to feed the young in the nest for 12–16 days, and if the female has a second brood, the male alone feeds the fledged first brood until they become independent. The diet includes berries, slugs, small snails, earthworms and insects.

The species is widespread in areas with scattered trees. It is absent only from parts of northern Scotland and the northern and western isles. Some birds, especially the young, fly south to the Continent for the winter.

Location	Behaviour	Sketch
Date		
Time		
Weather	Field marks	
Call		

Noisy scuffles are common among flocks of fieldfares as they feed.

Fieldfares feeding on pastures often mingle with redwings and golden plovers.

Chestnut back

Grey head

Adult fieldfare has a grey head and rump, chestnut back, black tail and spotted underparts. Birds are fond of windfall apples. Sexes are alike. 10 in. (25 cm).

In flight, fieldfares look pale in colour from below; flashes of white appear beneath the beating wings.

The fieldfare rises into the air almost vertically. The unmistakable grey rump contrasts with the black tail.

Oct.–Apr. visitor; has begun to nest in Scotland.

SITES GUIDE

The fieldfare nest is a strongly constructed cup of dried grass, moss and rootlets, lined with mud and insulated with fine dried grass.

The species may be seen at sites numbers: 7, 10, 15, 16, 23, 25, 26, 28, 34, 36-38, 40-43, 45-47, 51, 53, 54, 57.

Fieldfare *Turdus pilaris*

Large, loose flocks of fieldfares are a common feature of the winter landscape in Britain. They are noisy, clamorous birds often seen in pastures searching for seeds and small creatures such as spiders or centipedes, or on thick hawthorns attacking the bright red berries. Alternatively they may be seen flying overhead, sometimes in large flocks on their way to a communal roost, when their chattering 'chack-chack-chack' and occasional squeaking 'weeek' calls may be heard.

Both fieldfares and redwings are northern species of thrush. Few breed in this country, but large numbers arrive in autumn to spend the winter in a less severe climate than that of their native land.

Fieldfares nest in a variety of British habitats, including farmland, woodland edges, forestry plantations and moorland valleys. The breeding season depends on the latitude, starting in April in the south of the bird's range and as late as June in the north. Two clutches of five to six eggs are laid each year. The eggs, which are glossy and light blue, with reddish-brown speckles, are incubated by the female. For their 12–16 days in the nest the chicks are fed by both adults.

Location	Behaviour	Sketch
Date		
Time		
Weather	Field marks	
Call		

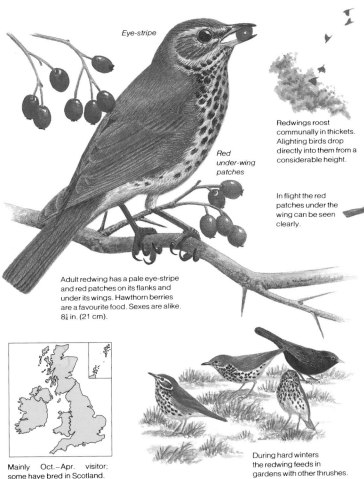

Eye-stripe

Red under-wing patches

Adult redwing has a pale eye-stripe and red patches on its flanks and under its wings. Hawthorn berries are a favourite food. Sexes are alike. 8¼ in. (21 cm).

Redwings roost communally in thickets. Alighting birds drop directly into them from a considerable height.

In flight the red patches under the wing can be seen clearly.

Rhododendrons are a favourite home for pairs nesting in Scotland.

Mainly Oct.–Apr. visitor; some have bred in Scotland.

During hard winters the redwing feeds in gardens with other thrushes.

Redwing *Turdus iliacus*

On clear, starry nights in September and October the careful listener may detect a thin, hissing 'seeeeip'-like sound at intervals overhead. It is the sign that redwings are in flight, calling to keep in contact with their fellows. They will have set out from northern Europe, where they breed, some hours before. Some will remain in Britain; others will continue further south. The severe winters of their breeding grounds mean that they must seek in warmer climes for their food – berries such as hawthorn, yew, holly and mountain ash, and invertebrates like worms, snails and spiders.

A few redwings breed in northern Scotland, in woodlands of birch, alder or pine, in spinneys, valleys, gullies among mountains or even in gardens. The nest is usually in a tree, against the trunk, or in a shrub; other nests may be in tree stumps or steep banks. The female builds the nest – a firm cup of dried grass, fine twigs and moss – between May and July.

The eggs are smooth and glossy, pale blue or greenish-blue in colour with fine specklings of reddish-brown. Incubation lasts for up to 15 days. The nestlings are fed by both parents for about two weeks in the nest, and for some time after they fledge.

Location	Behaviour	Sketch
Date		
Time		
Weather	Field marks	
Call		

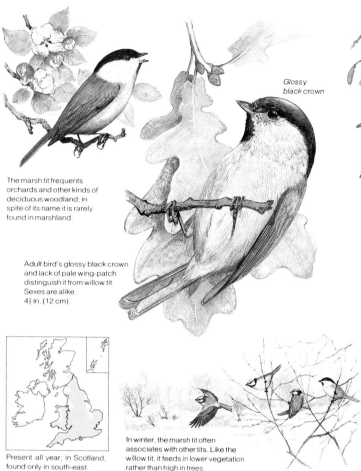

The marsh tit frequents orchards and other kinds of deciduous woodland; in spite of its name it is rarely found in marshland.

Adult bird's glossy black crown and lack of pale wing-patch distinguish it from willow tit. Sexes are alike. 4½ in. (12 cm).

Glossy black crown

Present all year; in Scotland, found only in south-east.

In winter, the marsh tit often associates with other tits. Like the willow tit, it feeds in lower vegetation rather than high in trees.

Juvenile bird has a browner crown than the adult; otherwise it is very similar to the young willow tit.

Marsh tit *Parus palustris*

From a distance, it is almost impossible to tell the marsh tit and the willow tit apart. On close inspection the marsh tit's black crown is glossy rather than sooty like the willow tit's. It also lacks the pale patch which the willow tit has on its wings. Yet no two British birds resemble each other more, and the only other way to distinguish them in the field is by their calls and songs.

The call of the marsh tit ranges from a distinctive 'pitchew' to a scolding 'chickabee-bee-bee-bee'. The willow tit has a loud 'tchay' and a high-pitched 'zee-zee-zee'. The marsh tit's song varies from a single note repeated over and over again, to a phrase such as 'pitchaweeoo'. One of the songs of the willow tit – 'chu-chu-chu' – is more melodious and warbling.

The marsh tit's mossy nest is built by the female, usually in a natural tree-hole, and forms a neat cup, lined with hair and a few feathers. Nesting usually begins in April or May and five to nine white eggs are normally laid. They are smooth, slightly glossy and have sparse purple-red or red-brown speckles. They take 13–17 days to hatch. Incubation is carried out by the female, fed on the nest by her partner. After fledging, the young remain dependent for a further week.

Location	Behaviour	Sketch
Date		
Time		
Weather	Field marks	
Call		

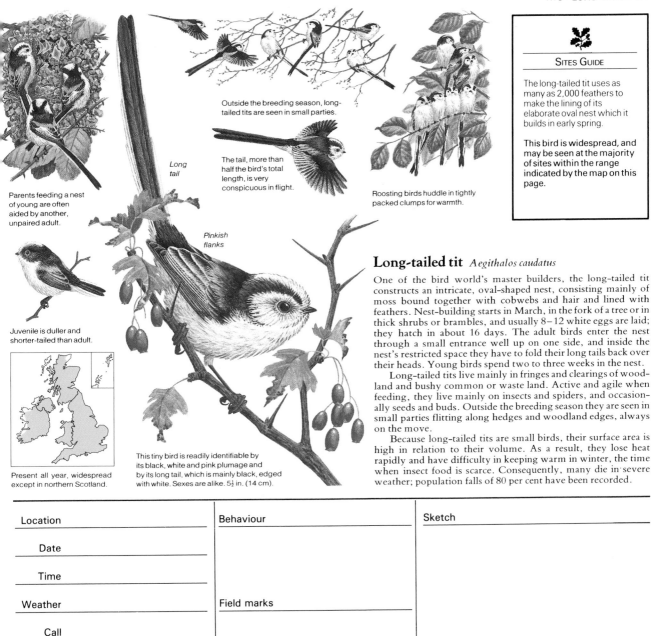

Parents feeding a nest of young are often aided by another, unpaired adult.

Juvenile is duller and shorter-tailed than adult.

Present all year, widespread except in northern Scotland.

Outside the breeding season, long-tailed tits are seen in small parties.

Long tail

The tail, more than half the bird's total length, is very conspicuous in flight.

Pinkish flanks

Roosting birds huddle in tightly packed clumps for warmth.

This tiny bird is readily identifiable by its black, white and pink plumage and by its long tail, which is mainly black, edged with white. Sexes are alike. 5½ in. (14 cm).

SITES GUIDE

The long-tailed tit uses as many as 2,000 feathers to make the lining of its elaborate oval nest which it builds in early spring.

This bird is widespread, and may be seen at the majority of sites within the range indicated by the map on this page.

Long-tailed tit *Aegithalos caudatus*

One of the bird world's master builders, the long-tailed tit constructs an intricate, oval-shaped nest, consisting mainly of moss bound together with cobwebs and hair and lined with feathers. Nest-building starts in March, in the fork of a tree or in thick shrubs or brambles, and usually 8–12 white eggs are laid; they hatch in about 16 days. The adult birds enter the nest through a small entrance well up on one side, and inside the nest's restricted space they have to fold their long tails back over their heads. Young birds spend two to three weeks in the nest.

Long-tailed tits live mainly in fringes and clearings of woodland and bushy common or waste land. Active and agile when feeding, they live mainly on insects and spiders, and occasionally seeds and buds. Outside the breeding season they are seen in small parties flitting along hedges and woodland edges, always on the move.

Because long-tailed tits are small birds, their surface area is high in relation to their volume. As a result, they lose heat rapidly and have difficulty in keeping warm in winter, the time when insect food is scarce. Consequently, many die in severe weather; population falls of 80 per cent have been recorded.

Location	Behaviour	Sketch
Date		
Time		
Weather	Field marks	
Call		

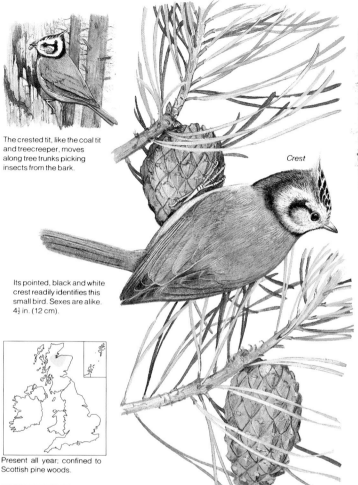

The crested tit, like the coal tit and treecreeper, moves along tree trunks picking insects from the bark.

Crest

Its pointed, black and white crest readily identifies this small bird. Sexes are alike. 4½ in. (12 cm).

Present all year; confined to Scottish pine woods.

Pine forests are a favourite habitat, though the birds may also be found in mixed woodland.

SITES GUIDE

In their first weeks of life the young crested tits in their tree-hole nest are fed by the male bird alone; later, both parents bring food.

The species may be seen at sites numbers: 55-57.

Crested tit *Parus cristatus*

A distinctive soft, rattling trill in the tree canopy of pine forest or mixed woodland gives away the presence of a flock of crested tits. But the call is not heard outside a relatively small area of the central Scottish Highlands, focused on the Spey Valley. For a species which frequents so much of Europe from Spain and Greece north to central Scandinavia, it is remarkable that the crested tit is absent from such large areas of apparently suitable habitat in the British Isles.

Since the crested tit is a very sedentary species, the lack of suitable food in winter may be a crucial factor in restricting its range and preventing it from colonising the enormous areas of new pine plantation that have been established in Britain.

The nest is usually built in a hole in a tree stump excavated by the female. It is a cup of moss and lichen lined with hair, wool and sometimes spiders' webs. A clutch may vary in size from four to eight eggs, or occasionally more. They are white, speckled with various shades of red or reddish–brown, and are incubated by the female for two to two and a half weeks before they hatch. The bird's diet consists of insects and their larvae, as well as pine seeds and berries.

Location _____

Date _____

Time _____

Weather _____

Call _____

Behaviour _____

Field marks _____

Sketch _____

Matt black crown

Adult willow tit is identified by pale wing-patch and the sooty, matt black feathers of its crown. Sexes are alike. 4½ in. (12 cm).

The willow tit often hunts for food in the lower levels of vegetation, but rarely lands on the ground.

Present all year; in Scotland, found only in south-west.

This species, like the crested tit, excavates its own nest holes, usually in the soft trunks of rotted alders, willows or birches.

SITES GUIDE

Once they have dug out their nest holes, willow tits carpet them with wood fibre, rabbit-down and frequently a few feathers.

The species may be seen at sites numbers: 2, 3, 6, 15, 18, 19, 26, 29, 31, 32, 35, 37, 40, 41, 43-45, 47, 51, 54.

Willow tit *Parus montanus*

Until 1897, the willow tit was thought not to be present in Britain, although it was widespread on the Continent. Then two ornithologists, Otto Kleinschmidt and Ernst Hartert, found the skins of two willow tits in a tray marked 'marsh tits' in the Bird Room of the British Museum of Natural History. The two skins had come from Hampstead, in North London, where the willow tits had been nesting.

Later that year, the Rothschild Museum at Tring, in Hertfordshire, acquired two willow tits from Finchley. Gradually it was realised that the bird was almost as common as the very similar marsh tit. Today, there are between 50,000 and 100,000 pairs of willow tits resident in Britain.

The willow tit favours damp woods with decaying trees such as the willow, the birch and the alder in which to build its nest. A normal clutch consists of six to nine smooth, glossy eggs. They are white with fine, red or reddish-brown speckles. The male feeds the female while she is incubating them. After about two weeks, the nestlings hatch and both parents tend them, bringing beakfuls of various insects, together with their eggs and larvae.

Location	Behaviour	Sketch
Date		
Time		
Weather	Field marks	
Call		

Blue
crown

White
face

Adult bird is identified by its bluish
upper parts and yellow underparts.
White face and bright blue crown are
also distinctive. Sexes are alike.
4½ in. (12 cm).

Blue tits readily use
nest-boxes, from
which they
immediately remove
the droppings of
their young.

Present all year; familiar and
widespread in Britain.

Brighter-coloured Continental birds
often reach southern Britain in
sudden migratory movements.

Young birds have yellow faces, and
remain together in groups for some time.

Birds are noisy and aggressive,
and may threaten each other
in squabbles over food.

SITES GUIDE

The blue tit displays great
resource in finding food, and
is well known for its habit of
pecking through milk bottle
tops.

This bird is widespread, and
may be seen at the majority
of sites within the range
indicated by the map on this
page.

Blue tit *Parus caeruleus*

Although the blue tit is chiefly a woodland bird – and feeds in the
tops of trees – it will visit garden bird-tables and amuse onlook-
ers with its lively, acrobatic behaviour. It is able to cling on to a
piece of suspended food at any angle, and eats a wide variety of
titbits. It may breed wherever there are areas of trees with holes
in which it can make its nest. The bottom of the nest-hole is
filled with moss, dried grass, dead leaves and wool, and the
nest-cup itself is lined with hair, feathers or down. Nest-boxes
can be put out for the blue tit, but the entrance hole should be too
small to admit the acquisitive house sparrow.

A clutch of usually 7–12 eggs is laid from mid-April to early
May. As the eggs are laid at daily intervals, and incubation
begins only when the clutch is almost complete, the hen bird
usually covers them with some nest lining if she has to leave
them for a while. The young are fed largely on caterpillars, and
remain in the nest for two to three weeks.

The blue tit has a large vocabulary of calls, though less so
than that of the great tit. Its song consists of two or three notes
followed by a rapid trill, which sounds like 'tee-tee-tee-
tississississississi'.

Location	Behaviour	Sketch
Date		
Time		
Weather	Field marks	
Call		

Coal tits are able to survive in prolonged periods of snow because they feed on insects living beneath the shelter of tree bark.

Black cap

White nape-patch

White nape-patch below a black cap distinguishes the coal tit, smallest of the seven tits breeding in Britain. It has greyish upper parts with a double white wing-bar and buff underparts. Sexes are alike. 4½ in. (12 cm).

Nesting coal tits may take over a disused rodent burrow as a site for building.

Present all year, mainly in conifer woods.

Juveniles have yellow head patches and underparts. The nape-patch and lack of a belly-stripe distinguish them from young great tits.

Coal tit *Parus ater*

Coniferous woodlands are the favourite home of the coal tit. But it can also be seen in deciduous or mixed woods, in gardens, orchards and, outside the breeding season, in hedgerows.

The coal tit, which is the smallest of all British tits, eats beetles, flies, moths and bugs – whether as eggs, larvae or adults – and spiders. It also feeds on plant food, such as weed seeds and conifer seeds, nut kernels and beech-mast, and will take food such as meat and suet scraps from bird tables. Except during breeding time, coal tits often feed in flocks, sometimes mixing with other species of tit.

The bird's nest is almost always in a hole, in a tree or tree-stump, in a wall or in a bank. Both sexes build the nest, using moss with a thick lining of hair and often feathers to produce a neat cup shape. The male feeds the female on the nest during her 14–16 days' incubation of the seven to nine eggs. The chicks leave the nest 16–19 days after hatching. They swiftly acquire the acrobatic skills characteristic of the tit family, and become independent after about two weeks. The call notes of the fully grown coal tit are mostly musical, thin and high-pitched – the commonest a rather plaintive 'tsee' and a 'tsooee'.

Location	Behaviour	Sketch
Date		
Time		
Weather	Field marks	
Call		

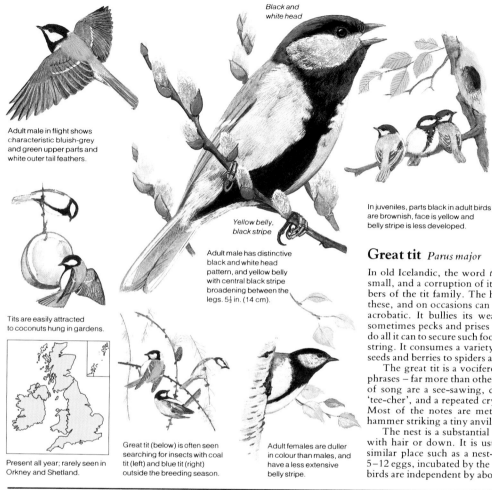

Adult male in flight shows characteristic bluish-grey and green upper parts and white outer tail feathers.

Tits are easily attracted to coconuts hung in gardens.

Present all year; rarely seen in Orkney and Shetland.

Great tit (below) is often seen searching for insects with coal tit (left) and blue tit (right) outside the breeding season.

Black and white head

Yellow belly, black stripe

Adult male has distinctive black and white head pattern, and yellow belly with central black stripe broadening between the legs. 5½ in. (14 cm).

Adult females are duller in colour than males, and have a less extensive belly stripe.

In juveniles, parts black in adult birds are brownish, face is yellow and belly stripe is less developed.

SITES GUIDE

Great tits start to breed in late March, in time for nestlings to be fed mainly on newly hatched moth caterpillars.

This bird is widespread, and may be seen at the majority of sites within the range indicated by the map on this page.

Great tit *Parus major*

In old Icelandic, the word *tittr* meant a small bird or anything small, and a corruption of it provided a fitting name for members of the tit family. The handsome great tit is the largest of these, and on occasions can be among the most aggressive and acrobatic. It bullies its weaker relatives; like the blue tit, it sometimes pecks and prises the tops off milk bottles; and it will do all it can to secure such food as a nut suspended from a piece of string. It consumes a variety of food, from spring buds, fruits, seeds and berries to spiders and household scraps.

The great tit is a vociferous bird and has scores of calls and phrases – far more than other tits studied. Its commonest forms of song are a see-sawing, double-noted 'tee-cher', 'tee-cher', 'tee-cher', and a repeated cry of 'pee-too', 'pee-too', 'pee-too'. Most of the notes are metallic and sound rather like a tiny hammer striking a tiny anvil.

The nest is a substantial cup of moss and a little grass lined with hair or down. It is usually sited in a tree or a wall, or a similar place such as a nest-box, letter-box or drainpipe. The 5–12 eggs, incubated by the female, hatch in a fortnight. Young birds are independent by about four weeks old.

Location	Behaviour	Sketch
Date		
Time		
Weather	Field marks	
Call		

In winter the nuthatch often associates with tits, especially the great tit and blue tit.

Blue-grey upper parts

The nuthatch places nuts such as acorns in cracks in the bark; it then hammers them open with its bill.

Present all year in areas where there are large trees.

By adding mud to the entrance the adult bird adjusts the size of its nesting hole.

Adult bird is plump and short-tailed, with blue-grey upper parts, buff underparts and reddish flanks. It has a strong, pointed bill and black eye-stripe. Sexes are alike. 5½ in. (14 cm).

The bird hops obliquely up and down a trunk, gripping with one foot and bracing itself with the other.

SITES GUIDE

A nuthatch may be spotted emerging cautiously from its nesting hole in a tree trunk; the bird also nests in boxes and walls.

The species may be seen at sites numbers: 1, 3, 4, 7-11, 14, 16, 17, 19, 21, 22, 25, 27, 28, 31-33, 35-39, 41, 44-47 and 53.

Nuthatch *Sitta europaea*

A loud 'chwit', repeated many times as the bird scrutinises a tree-trunk, or a rapid trilling 'chirirriri', can be the first clue to the presence of a nuthatch. It is the only member of its family to breed in Britain, and inhabits deciduous woodland, large gardens and parkland.

The original name for the nuthatch was 'nut-hack', derived from the bird's habit of fixing nuts in a crevice of the tree's bark and hacking them open with its bill to find the kernel. It eats hazel and beech nuts, acorns, seeds and also insects that it picks from the bark. The nuthatch is the only bird that can hop down tree trunks as easily as it hops up.

Nuthatches breed in holes in trees or walls, or in nest-boxes, from late April to early May. They make the entrance and any neighbouring cracks smaller by filling them with mud which hardens to a rock-like consistency. The bottom of the hole is usually lined with small fragments of bark or dried leaves which are used to cover the eggs. The average clutch, laid at daily intervals, numbers six to nine white eggs. These are boldly blotched, especially at the larger end, with reddish or purplish spots. The female incubates the eggs for about two weeks.

Location	Behaviour	Sketch
Date		
Time		
Weather	Field marks	
Call		

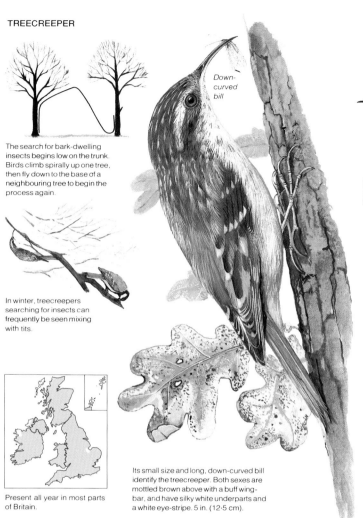

The search for bark-dwelling insects begins low on the trunk. Birds climb spirally up one tree, then fly down to the base of a neighbouring tree to begin the process again.

In winter, treecreepers searching for insects can frequently be seen mixing with tits.

Down-curved bill

The flight is slightly undulating, usually over short distances only. The long tail, divided into points at the end, shows up clearly.

Present all year in most parts of Britain.

Its small size and long, down-curved bill identify the treecreeper. Both sexes are mottled brown above with a buff wing-bar, and have silky white underparts and a white eye-stripe. 5 in. (12·5 cm).

SITES GUIDE

Treecreepers' nests are usually sited behind loose bark or ivy on old trees, or in large cracks in the trunk. Two broods are reared each year.

This bird is widespread, and may be seen at the majority of sites within the range indicated by the map on this page.

Treecreeper *Certhia familiaris*

Large claws and a stiff, fairly long tail enable the treecreeper to creep jerkily up tree trunks. It makes short hops with both feet at once, and uses its tail as a prop. As the central pair of tail feathers are not moulted until all others have been renewed, there is always sufficient support for climbing. Because it cannot descend in the same way, the bird flies from the upper trunk down to the base of the next tree.

Weevils, beetles, earwigs, small moths, woodlice, spiders and their eggs – all these form part of the treecreeper's diet. Its nest is a loose cup of moss, roots and dried grass on a base of small twigs, and is lined with feathers, wool and bark fragments. Here the female lays three to nine, but most often six, white eggs, speckled red at the large end. Once the chicks hatch, both parents feed them for 14–16 days. On leaving the nest they can climb competently, but are weak fliers at first.

The song of the treecreeper is thin and high-pitched, the note sequence starting slowly and accelerating to a flourish. Its call note is a shrill 'tseee'. The rare short-toed treecreeper, common on the Continent, is distinguished by its light brown flanks and less-distinct white eye-stripe.

Location	Behaviour	Sketch
Date		
Time		
Weather	Field marks	
Call		

Chestnut crown

Holes in old fruit trees are popular nesting sites. Nest-boxes may be used.

In flight, tree sparrows give a high, distinctive 'teck-teck' call.

SITES GUIDE

Like the house sparrow, the tree sparrow is an eager and boisterous bather in hot weather, using any puddles it can find.

The species may be seen at sites numbers: 16, 18, 20, 23, 25, 26, 28, 34, 37, 40-43, 45, 47, 52, 53.

After the breeding season, tree sparrows may search for food with finches and house sparrows.

Its all-chestnut crown and the black patches on its cheeks distinguish the tree sparrow from the male house sparrow. It is also slightly smaller. Males, females and juveniles are similarly marked. 5½ in. (14 cm).

Present all year. Birds from Continent also winter here.

Courting birds take turns in running towards each other, tail erect and bill thrust straight out. The watching bird 'bows' to its partner.

Tree sparrow *Passer montanus*

Country cousin to the house sparrow, the tree sparrow is a bird of open woodlands and orchards, feeding mainly on weed seeds. Its distribution is dependent to some extent on the availability of suitable nesting sites. It is rare in some parts, including, surprisingly, the New Forest, Hampshire. In most of Britain it is quite common, although populations fluctuate mysteriously, building up over a few years then rapidly decreasing. In recent years there has been a considerable increase after a period of decline.

Breeding, usually in colonies, begins any time from late April to late May, or even June in the north. Both birds build an untidy nest of dried grass or straw, forming a deep cup, and if the site is open they may add a domed roof. The hen usually lays four to six eggs, white or pale grey and boldly speckled with purplish-brown or grey.

The parent birds take turns to incubate the eggs, which hatch after 11–14 days, and both feed the chicks during their two weeks or so in the nest. They may raise two or three broods each season. The tree sparrow is one of the few species in which juveniles progressively moult all their plumage, including the flight feathers, in late summer.

Location	Behaviour	Sketch
Date		
Time		
Weather	Field marks	
Call		

The female house sparrow is a duller brown than the male, and lacks the grey crown and black bib. The white wing-bars are less distinct.

Young birds beg for food from their parents by holding their bodies low and quivering their wings.

Grey crown

The streaked brown back of the adult house sparrow is a familiar sight around most cities, towns and villages. Its grey crown distinguishes the male from the more lightly built tree sparrow. 5¾ in. (14·5 cm).

Birds often dust-bathe in suitable spots on open ground in high summer.

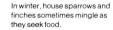

In winter, house sparrows and finches sometimes mingle as they seek food.

Present all year throughout the British Isles.

Nests are domed structures of straw and feathers when built in hedges; but in cities and towns an untidily lined hole in a building or tree may suffice.

House sparrow *Passer domesticus*

Ever since man began to build houses, this sparrow has partly depended upon him and his settlements for food and shelter. It is an intelligent bird and has adapted to major changes in the environment; for example, feeding off man's large grain fields and searching out nesting places in warm, sheltered hollows and ledges of his buildings. But not all nests are in buildings, occasionally they are found in hedges or ivy-clad trees.

Although the house sparrow is possibly the most familiar of British birds, it is not as numerous as the chaffinch, blackbird or wren. From March to August, three broods of from three to five young are quite frequent. The greyish-white eggs are covered with dark grey and greyish-brown speckles. The chicks hatch after 11–14 days and can fly reasonably well in another two weeks or so.

The most common call of the house sparrow is a rather persistent, rattling 'chissup' or 'chee-ip', repeated endlessly on rooftop, guttering, or garden trellis. A noticeable feature of the bird's courtship display is when several males, chirping noisily, crowd round a female who raises her bill and tail, droops her wings and pecks at them.

Location	Behaviour	Sketch
Date		
Time		
Weather	Field marks	
Call		

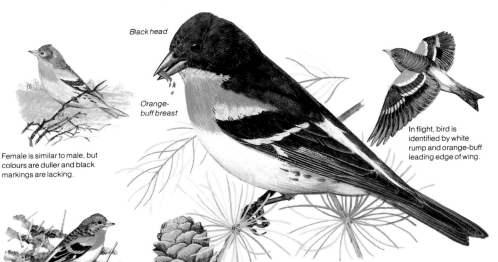

Black head

Orange-buff breast

In flight, bird is identified by white rump and orange-buff leading edge of wing.

Female is similar to male, but colours are duller and black markings are lacking.

Male in winter may resemble female, but usually keeps some black markings on head and back.

Adult male in breeding plumage, which may still be seen in early autumn or late spring. Head and back are black; breast and shoulders orange-buff. Black bill turns yellow in winter. 5¾ in. (14·5 cm).

Mainly Oct.–Apr. visitor; others rest during migration.

Bramblings often flock with other species such as chaffinches and greenfinches in winter, seeking nuts and seeds.

Brambling *Fringilla montifringilla*

Isolated cases of the brambling breeding in England and Scotland have been recorded, but this bird is for the most part only a winter visitor to Britain from breeding grounds in Scandinavia and northern Russia. The number of visitors that come varies widely, depending on the amount of food available in their cold northern latitudes, and on the severity of the winter there.

Immigrants normally arrive from the end of September to the middle of November, and stay until March, April or even later. Breeding birds choose birch or mixed woodland in which to nest. Clutches of four to five eggs are laid in a nest that is a rounded cup of grasses, lined with hair and feathers like that of the chaffinch, a bird so closely related to the brambling that the two birds have been known to interbreed.

The brambling's winter food includes weed seeds, pine seeds, berries, grain and in particular beech mast – fallen beech nuts. The likeliest places to find bramblings, therefore, are beech woods, stubble fields and yards where grain is stacked. A hoarse, monotonous 'diree' call, sometimes interspersed with a harsh rattling, is probably used to assert territorial rights. The note uttered in flight is a quiet, rapid 'chucc-chucc-chucc'.

Location	Behaviour	Sketch
Date		
Time		
Weather	Field marks	
Call		

Slate-blue crown

In flight, white wing-bar and shoulder-patch are distinctive.

In winter, chaffinches often flock with other finch species such as bramblings and greenfinches.

Pink-brown below

Adult male is unmistakable, with slate-blue crown and neck, chestnut back, pinkish-brown underparts and greenish rump. 6 in. (15 cm).

Present all year; joined by winter migrants.

Birds display aggression when food is short.

SITES GUIDE

Chaffinches nest in hedgerows, bushes and tree-forks, building a neat cup of grass, moss and lichens, lined with hair.

This bird is widespread, and may be seen at the majority of sites within the range indicated by the map on this page.

Females lack males' bright colours, but have same wing pattern.

Chaffinch *Fringilla coelebs*

It is estimated that there may be as many as seven million pairs of chaffinches in the British Isles, making it one of our most widespread and common birds. Even so, the chaffinch population has gradually decreased since the 1950s, due partly to the increasing use of toxic seed dressings and perhaps partly also to the disappearance of hedges in some areas. The bird exists mainly on weed seeds taken from the ground, and insects.

Chaffinches are mostly found in mature, deciduous woods; but they also abound in gardens, parks, orchards and farmland where there is scrub and bushes. Breeding starts in April or May. Usually four to five bluish or browny-white eggs, sometimes spotted, are laid and incubated by the female for 11–13 days. Both birds tend the young, which fly in 12–15 days.

The song is a loud, jangling affair which starts slowly, accelerates down the scale, and usually ends with an exuberant flourish of notes. The actual detail of the song varies greatly from bird to bird, and there are even distinct regional 'dialects' in different parts of Britain. The entire song normally lasts for about four or five seconds and is repeated up to five or ten times a minute. The alarm call is a loud and persistent 'pink, pink, pink'.

Location	Behaviour	Sketch
Date		
Time		
Weather	Field marks	
Call		

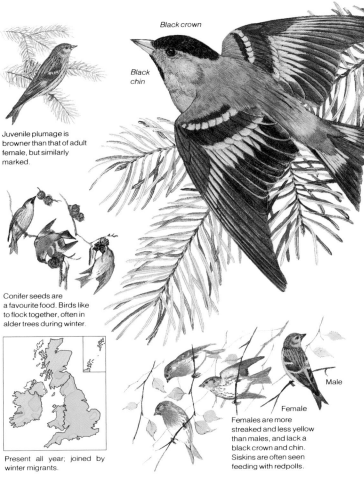

Black crown

Black chin

Juvenile plumage is browner than that of adult female, but similarly marked.

Conifer seeds are a favourite food. Birds like to flock together, often in alder trees during winter.

Present all year; joined by winter migrants.

Adult male has yellow-green rump and yellow tail-patch, like greenfinch. But it is smaller, and differs in having black crown and chin and different wing pattern. 4½ in. (12 cm).

Male

Female

Females are more streaked and less yellow than males, and lack a black crown and chin. Siskins are often seen feeding with redpolls.

Sites Guide

The siskin's nesting site is usually in a conifer tree, towards the end of a branch and at least 15ft (4-5m) above the ground.

The species may be seen at sites numbers: 2, 3, 6, 10, 22, 23, 26-28, 34, 39, 41, 43, 46, 47, 51, 54-57.

Siskin *Carduelis spinus*

The 20th-century practice of pine-planting in Britain has greatly benefited the siskin, which depends heavily upon the seeds of pines and spruce for food in spring and early summer. At one time the species was confined to the pine forests of the Scottish Highlands, but during the last 130 years it has spread widely.

The bird's flight calls are a high-pitched and squeaky 'tsys-ing' and a wheezy 'tsooeet'. The song is a sweet, musical and varied twittering refrain. It is delivered from a tree or during song flight, when the male slowly circles the tree tops on slow, deliberate wing-beats, with plumage fluffed-up and tail fanned. Both partners take part in a fast-moving display flight, in which the male rises to a considerable height with tail spread and wings quivering rapidly, and the female follows close behind.

The siskin's nest usually consists of small, lichen-covered twigs bound with grass, moss, plant fibres and wool. It is lined with finer materials such as hair and thistledown. In April or May the female lays usually three to five very pale blue speckled eggs, which hatch in two weeks. The young spend about two weeks in the nest, fed by the male for the first week, after which the female shares in collecting food for the chicks.

Location	Behaviour	Sketch
Date		
Time		
Weather	Field marks	
Call		

Male in song flight display flits and weaves erratically among tree-tops.

Wing and tail patterns are distinctive in flight.

Pink bill

Adult female is duller in colour, with faintly streaked underparts. Bird collects nesting materials of twigs, moss or roots.

Juvenile bird, more heavily streaked than adult female, receives food regurgitated by parents.

Yellow tail edge

Adult male has bright yellow wing-patch and tail edges. Seeds are cracked with characteristic pink bill. 5¾ in. (14·5 cm).

Present all year; sedentary, near human settlements.

Serin
Serinus serinus

This bird has bred in Britain on rare occasions since 1967. It is smaller than the green-finch – about 4¾ in. (12 cm) long – and its plumage is much yellower and more streaked.

Sites Guide

Vigorous bathers, greenfinches flock to urban gardens where there is water, particularly in dry summer conditions.

The species may be seen at sites numbers: 2, 4, 10, 14-21, 23, 25, 26, 28, 34, 36-38, 41-47, 52, 53.

Greenfinch *Carduelis chloris*

Almost any area with trees and bushes, except dense woodland, will harbour greenfinches. In gardens, woodland edges, copses and plantations their olive-green plumage can be seen, set off admirably by bright yellow wing and tail flashes.

While hardly the star of any dawn chorus, the greenfinch's song is nonetheless pleasant: a loud, rapid twittering on one note, followed by four or five musical notes – 'tew, tew, tew, tew, tew' – then a pause sometimes followed by a single 'greeee'. The song may be delivered from a bush or tree-top perch, or during a display flight high in a floppy, bat-like flight with slow, exaggerated wing-beats. When disturbed the bird flies off with a quiet 'chi-chi-chi-chi'.

Greenfinches start to breed in late April or early May. The nest is a bulky cup of twiglets, plant stems and moss, lined with rootlets, hair, fine stems and occasionally a few feathers. Several nests sometimes appear in one bush. The eggs, usually four to six, are greyish-white to pale greenish-blue with a sparse speckling of reddish-brown, black or lilac. They hatch in two weeks and the young spend about two weeks in the nest. With two or three broods a year, nestlings may be seen as late as September.

Location _____

Date _____

Time _____

Weather _____

Call _____

Behaviour _____

Field marks _____

Sketch

Juvenile birds lack any red colouring and have yellower bills than adults.

Redpolls are often seen by ponds, where they like to drink and bathe.

Most birds stay all year; some migrate, others visit.

Red forehead

Black chin

Pink breast

Adult male in summer plumage has red forehead, black chin and pink breast and rump. Adult female generally lacks pink breast and rump. 4½–6 in. (12–15 cm).

Native bird

Northern visitor

Larger, paler redpolls from northern Europe and Greenland may visit Britain in winter.

In winter, males have less pink on breast and rump. Birds feed in flocks on alder and birch seeds, often mixing with siskins.

Redpolls eat tree and plant seeds. Both sexes have buff-coloured double wing-bars.

SITES GUIDE

Silver birch trees and gorse bushes are popular nesting sites for redpolls. They often nest in loose-knit colonies.

The species may be seen at sites numbers: 2, 10, 14, 16, 18, 20-23, 26, 27, 36, 39, 41-43, 45-47, 54-56.

Redpoll *Acanthis flammea*

Conifers, alders and birches are the favourite habitat of the redpoll. The population has swelled markedly in the last 35 years with the increase in conifer planting, and often overflows from woodlands to hedgerows and gardens with suitable vegetation.

Usually, the first indication of the redpoll's presence is its distinctive flight call, a rattling, bell-like 'ching, ching, ching'. Like most finches, its flight is undulating. It also has an unusual display flight – a series of loops and circles with slow wing-beats and occasional glides – sometimes performed by several males together. The alarm call is a musical, plaintive 'tsooeet'.

Redpolls start to breed at the end of April in the south. Nesting sites vary from low bushes to high tree branches, and the nest is a small, rather untidy cup of twigs, dried grass and plant stems neatly lined with hair, thistledown and occasionally feathers. The four or five eggs are whitish–blue finely speckled with lilac and purple-brown, and the female incubates them for 10–13 days. Both parents tend the downy, dark grey nestlings for about a fortnight until they are fledged, and then for a short while afterwards. The redpoll's diet of seeds is sometimes supplemented by small insects and their larvae.

Location	Behaviour	Sketch
Date		
Time		
Weather	Field marks	
Call		

Yellow
wing-bar

Broad yellow bar
on black wing and
white rump help
identify bird in flight.

Red
face

Adult bird has red face, black and
white head and broad yellow wing-bar.
Sexes are similar. 4¾ in. (12 cm).

Juvenile birds lack much of
the adult's colourful marking;
they are darker brown,
streaked with buff.

Some birds stay all year;
others go south in winter.

Flocks are often seen bathing
together in summer.

SITES GUIDE

Goldfinches favour orchards
as breeding areas. The
female sits on the eggs in the
nest for about two weeks.

The species may be seen at
sites numbers: 2, 4, 7, 10, 12-
14, 16, 18-21, 23, 26, 28, 34,
36, 37, 40, 41, 43, 44, 45, 47
and 53.

Goldfinch *Carduelis carduelis*

A flock of goldfinches is called a 'charm', and there is no better
way of describing these delightful birds. It is a joy to watch a
charm feeding on thistles or groundsel, delicately picking out
the seeds, and periodically moving – with dancing flight – from
plant to plant. The pleasure is enhanced by their tinkling,
bell-like calls. The song is a pretty, liquid twittering – an
elaborate version of the flight notes.

The goldfinch is one of the most popular small birds among
cage-bird enthusiasts and birdwatchers alike. It is found in
neglected farmland, gardens and open areas with scattered trees.
There it finds its preferred diet of annual weed seeds, supplemented by insects. The nest, built by the female, is a neat and
delicately woven cup of plant material, including thistledown. It
is usually well hidden in the upper branches of small trees.

Usually four to six eggs are laid from late April to early May.
They are a very pale, bluish-white with a few streaks of reddish-
brown. The chicks spend about two weeks in the nest, are fed by
regurgitation, and depend on their parents for about a week after
fledging. During that time they make a constant twitter of
contact calls with the adult birds.

Location	Behaviour	Sketch
Date		
Time		
Weather	Field marks	
Call		

Black cap

In flight the male's black cap, white rump and white wing-bar are conspicuous.

Adult male is unmistakable with its red underparts, black cap, grey upper parts and striking white rump. 6 in. (15 cm).

White rump

Adult female has the same basic plumage as the male, but underparts are dull salmon-pink. Bullfinches are notorious for attacking flowering fruit trees.

Present all year; absent from extreme north and north-west.

Juveniles are mostly brownish, but have the adult's white rump.

Bullfinch *Pyrrhula pyrrhula*

Although one of Britain's prettiest birds, the bullfinch can also be one of the most destructive. It attacks the buds of fruit trees and flowering shrubs, and at times the damage is so costly that fruit growers are permitted to destroy the birds by shooting or trapping.

The nest, a distinctive structure of fine twigs, moss and lichen lined with black or blackish-brown rootlets, varies in size from a shallow platform to a bulky cup. The four or five eggs are pale greenish-blue with dark purplish-brown spots and streaks. They are incubated for 12–14 days mainly by the female, which is fed during this time by the male. Both parents feed the hatched young in the nest by regurgitation from special throat pouches. Young birds fly after 12–18 days. Two and sometimes three broods may be raised each year.

The call note, often the only clue to a bullfinch's presence, is a soft, piping 'dew', repeated at intervals. It has considerable carrying power but is often difficult to locate. The fledged young have a similar call though less pure, louder and more persistent. The bullfinch does not have a proper song, though at close quarters a faint, creaky warble can be heard.

Location	Behaviour	Sketch
Date		
Time		
Weather	Field marks	
Call		

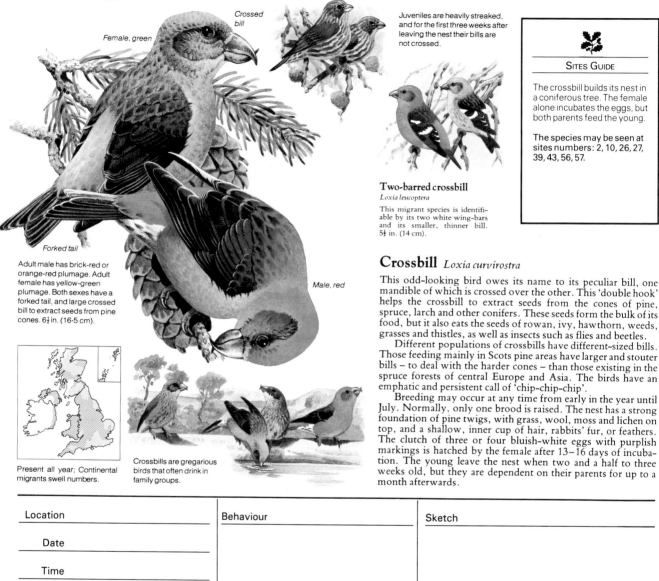

Female, green

Crossed bill

Juveniles are heavily streaked, and for the first three weeks after leaving the nest their bills are not crossed.

Forked tail

Adult male has brick-red or orange-red plumage. Adult female has yellow-green plumage. Both sexes have a forked tail, and large crossed bill to extract seeds from pine cones. 6¼ in. (16·5 cm).

Male, red

Present all year; Continental migrants swell numbers.

Crossbills are gregarious birds that often drink in family groups.

Two-barred crossbill
Loxia leucoptera

This migrant species is identifiable by its two white wing-bars and its smaller, thinner bill. 5¼ in. (14 cm).

Sites Guide

The crossbill builds its nest in a coniferous tree. The female alone incubates the eggs, but both parents feed the young.

The species may be seen at sites numbers: 2, 10, 26, 27, 39, 43, 56, 57.

Crossbill *Loxia curvirostra*

This odd-looking bird owes its name to its peculiar bill, one mandible of which is crossed over the other. This 'double hook' helps the crossbill to extract seeds from the cones of pine, spruce, larch and other conifers. These seeds form the bulk of its food, but it also eats the seeds of rowan, ivy, hawthorn, weeds, grasses and thistles, as well as insects such as flies and beetles.

Different populations of crossbills have different-sized bills. Those feeding mainly in Scots pine areas have larger and stouter bills – to deal with the harder cones – than those existing in the spruce forests of central Europe and Asia. The birds have an emphatic and persistent call of 'chip-chip-chip'.

Breeding may occur at any time from early in the year until July. Normally, only one brood is raised. The nest has a strong foundation of pine twigs, with grass, wool, moss and lichen on top, and a shallow, inner cup of hair, rabbits' fur, or feathers. The clutch of three or four bluish-white eggs with purplish markings is hatched by the female after 13–16 days of incubation. The young leave the nest when two and a half to three weeks old, but they are dependent on their parents for up to a month afterwards.

Location	Behaviour	Sketch
Date		
Time		
Weather	Field marks	
Call		

Large head

Large bill

Birds in flight appear large-headed and short-tailed. Wing and tail pattern is prominent.

Juveniles are yellower than adults, lack a black bib, and have a yellow throat-patch. Birds of all ages visit ponds regularly.

Aggression is frequently displayed while feeding.

Adult male appears heavy-headed, and has a mainly chestnut body, with black and white wings. The powerful bill is used to open seeds. 7 in. (18 cm).

Female

The bird raids vegetable gardens in early morning to tear open pea-pods and feed on the peas.

Present all year; sometimes seen outside breeding range.

Male

Hawfinches are frequently seen in small parties feeding in hornbeams. Females are duller than males.

Sites Guide

Hawfinch nests are bulky, made from twigs and moss lined with roots and grass. They are often placed high in fruit trees.

The species may be seen at sites numbers: 2, 10, 16, 18, 19, 25-27, 41, 43, 45-47, 51.

Hawfinch *Coccothraustes coccothraustes*

Any ornithologist, who, during bird-ringing studies, is lucky enough to catch a hawfinch will handle the bird with considerable respect. It is quite capable of removing a neat chunk from his finger, in much the same way as an apple-corer removes the core from an apple. The heavy, conical bill of the hawfinch is designed to crack open such hard seeds as cherry stones, to get at the edible kernel inside. The bones of its bill and palate and its jaw muscles are especially powerful.

An abrupt, explosive 'tik' is occasionally a clue to the bird's presence high overhead. The hawfinch, however, is a shy bird and is difficult to find. The species is mainly confined to England and a few places in Wales, where it favours deciduous or mixed woodlands, old, well-wooded parks and gardens, and bushy areas scattered with trees. These places provide a wide variety of seeds and kernels, including beechmast, maple, hawthorn, yew, pea and sloe. The bird supplements its diet with buds in the spring and insects in the summer.

In late April or early May the hawfinch begins to breed. It usually lays a single clutch of five greenish or bluish eggs, finely stippled with black. They hatch after 9–14 days of incubation.

Location	Behaviour	Sketch
Date		
Time		
Weather	Field marks	
Call		

Pairs of reed buntings are often found in drier areas, but never far from water.

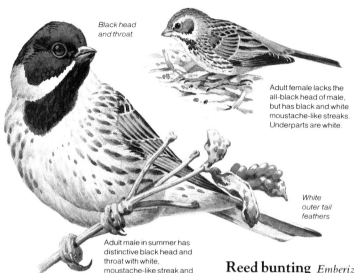

Black head and throat

Adult male in summer has distinctive black head and throat with white, moustache-like streak and nape. The upper body is rich brown streaked with black. White outer tail feathers are conspicuous. 6 in. (15 cm).

Adult female lacks the all-black head of male, but has black and white moustache-like streaks. Underparts are white.

White outer tail feathers

Male in winter lacks most of its black plumage. The male bird frequently flicks its wings and tail, or spreads its tail showing white outer feathers.

Present all year; Continental birds on passage.

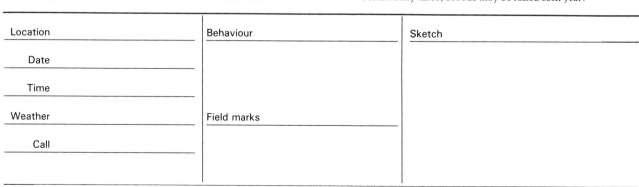

Reed buntings often associate with other birds such as yellowhammers in stubble fields while searching for winter food.

Reed bunting *Emberiza schoeniclus*

With its white collar and moustachial streak and black head, the male reed bunting is reminiscent of a Victorian Guards officer. Clinging to a swaying reed, the bird delivers its chirruping song, a simple 'cheep-cheep-cheep-chizzup', with an occasional flick of the tail before flying jerkily to another clump of reeds.

The reed bunting is less appropriately named than it once was, for in recent years it has extended its range from the reed beds of fenland and river bank to drier places such as farm hedgerows, downland scrub and forestry plantations. In some areas it has been seen visiting gardens to feed along with house sparrows and greenfinches. Its favourite breeding grounds, however, are still the marshy places and riversides, where the female builds her nest in a tussock of rush or among dense vegetation close to the ground.

The nest is a cup of grass and moss lined with fine grasses, reed flowers and hair. A clutch usually numbers four or five eggs, brownish-olive or buff with a few streaks and spots of blackish-brown. The chicks hatch in two weeks and spend about two weeks in the nest, tended by both parents. Two, or occasionally three, broods may be raised each year.

Location	Behaviour	Sketch
Date		
Time		
Weather	Field marks	
Call		

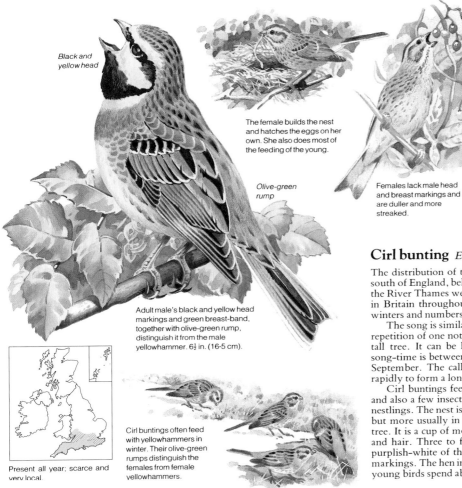

Black and yellow head

The female builds the nest and hatches the eggs on her own. She also does most of the feeding of the young.

Olive-green rump

Females lack male head and breast markings and are duller and more streaked.

Adult male's black and yellow head markings and green breast-band, together with olive-green rump, distinguish it from the male yellowhammer. 6½ in. (16·5 cm).

Present all year; scarce and very local.

Cirl buntings often feed with yellowhammers in winter. Their olive-green rumps distinguish the females from female yellowhammers.

SITES GUIDE

Cirl buntings' nest sites may be at either ground level or in tree branches.

The species may be seen at site number: 10.

Cirl bunting *Emberiza cirlus*

The distribution of the cirl bunting in Britain is limited to the south of England, below a line drawn from the Severn estuary to the River Thames west of London. Although the bird is resident in Britain throughout the year, it suffers considerably in cold winters and numbers become depleted.

The song is similar to that of the lesser whitethroat, a rattling repetition of one note delivered from a bush, telegraph wire or tall tree. It can be heard throughout the year, but the peak song-time is between the end of February and the beginning of September. The call note is a short 'sit', sometimes repeated rapidly to form a longer 'si–si–si–si–sit'.

Cirl buntings feed mainly on grass seeds, corn and berries, and also a few insects, which form the bulk of the food for the nestlings. The nest is built by the hen, sometimes on the ground but more usually in a thick bush or in the lower branches of a tree. It is a cup of moss, grass and rootlets lined with fine grass and hair. Three to four eggs are laid, similar in colour to the purplish–white of those of the yellowhammer but with bolder markings. The hen incubates them for about two weeks, and the young birds spend about two weeks in the nest.

Location	Behaviour	Sketch
Date		
Time		
Weather	Field marks	
Call		

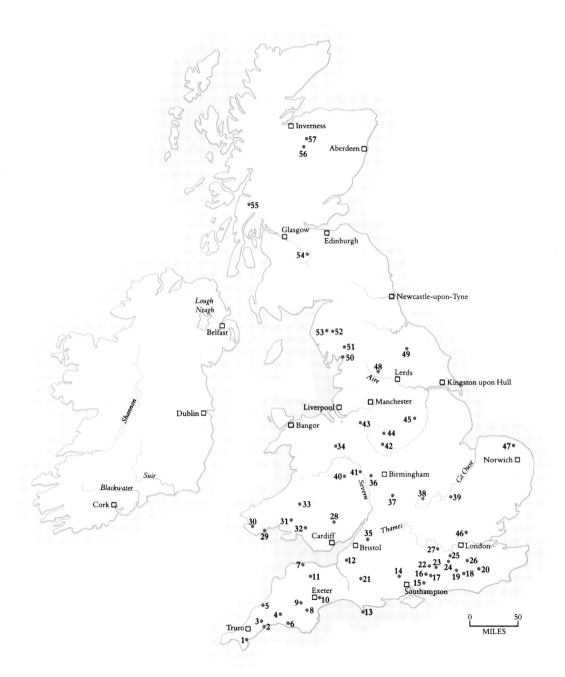

Inverness □
• 57
56 •   Aberdeen □

• 55

Glasgow □
Edinburgh □
54 •

□ Newcastle-upon-Tyne

Lough
Neagh
Belfast □

53 • • 52
• 51
50 •
48 •   Leeds □
Aire
□ Kingston upon Hull
49 •

Dublin □
Liverpool □   □ Manchester

Bangor □
• 43
• 45
44 •
• 34
42 •
• 47
Norwich □

40 • • 41   □ Birmingham
Severn
36
Gt Ouse

33 •
• 37
38 •
• 39

30 •
31 •   28 •
32 •   Cardiff □
35 •   *Thames*
46 •

29 •
Bristol □
London □

Shannon

Suir

Blackwater
Cork □

7 •
12 •
27 •
25 •
14 •   22 • 23 •
16 • 24 •
26 •
20 •
• 11
21 •
17 •
19 • 18 •
15 •
Exeter □
Southampton □

9 •
5 •   10 •
4 •   8 •
13 •

Truro □   3 •
2 •   6 •
1 •

0   50
MILES

96

The Sites

A descriptive gazetteer of places around Britain to see the birds on pages 12-95.

(In this *Nature Notebook* there are no Irish sites: almost all the best birdwatching there with public access is on coastal or wetland locations.)

Order

The sites are featured in a special order, designed for ease of reference. They follow each other in a sequence determined by the Ordnance Survey's grid reference system, which works from west to east, and from south to north. The first sites described are those in Cornwall, in other words those furthest west and furthest south; the last sites described on mainland Britain are in north-east Scotland.

For additional ease of reference, the sites are, however, grouped in regions and counties, and this framework takes precedence over the order required by the grid system; so that, for example, all the sites in Wales, from south to north, are listed together; then the list continues, starting afresh with the south-west corner of the Midlands, ie Gloucestershire.

Location of sites

Each site is described in terms of access from a nearby major road or town, or other major landmark. In England, Scotland and Wales, the number of the Ordnance Survey Landranger sheet (scale 1:50 000) on which the site occurs is also given, together with a grid reference number for exact and speedy location of the site on the map. Full directions on how to read a numerical grid reference are given on all Landranger sheets. Six-figure grid reference numbers are accurate to the nearest hundred metres and these are given where possible; however, it is sometimes more appropriate to quote a four-figure grid reference, accurate to the nearest kilometre, when a large area is in question. A quality motoring map will, in most cases, be adequate to locate a given site generally; the *Ordnance Survey Motoring Atlas* at a scale of 3 miles (5 km) to one inch (2.5 cm) is highly suitable and has the advantage of using the national grid reference system. The larger scale Landranger mapping is invaluable once you have arrived, for it shows public footpaths and details enabling you to make the most of an area.

Bird names in bold type

Bird names in **bold** are those which are featured in the identification section, pages 12-95.

Ornithological terms

A glossary explaining the meaning of ornithological terms is on pages 124-5.

KEY TO MAP

1 Helford River
2 Fowey
3 Lanhydrock
4 Cotehele
5 Boscastle Harbour and Valency Valley
6 Plym Bridge Woods
7 Lynmouth
8 Parke, Bovey Tracey
9 Castle Drogo
10 Killerton
11 Barle Valley
12 Cheddar Cliffs
13 Portland Bill
14 Mottisfont Abbey
15 Queen Elizabeth Country Park
16 Selborne Hill
17 Durford Heath
18 Wakehurst Place

19 Nymans Gardens
20 Nap Wood
21 Stourhead
22 Alice Holt Forest
23 Hindhead
24 Holmwood Common
25 Box Hill
26 Limpsfield Common and The Chart
27 Virginia Water
28 Sugar Loaf
29 Colby Estate
30 Little Milford
31 Castle Woods
32 Dinas Hill
33 Henrhyd Falls and Craigllech Woods
34 Erdigg
35 Newark Park
36 Clent Hills
37 Charlecote Park
38 Salcey Forest

39 The Lodge, Sandy
40 Wenlock Edge
41 Dudmaston Estate
42 Hawksmoor Nature Reserve
43 Styal Country Park
44 Dovedale
45 Clumber Park
46 Epping Forest
47 Blickling
48 Bolton Abbey Woods
49 Whitestone Cliff
50 Eaves and Waterslack Woods
51 Sizergh Castle
52 Ullswater: Glencoyne Park and Woods
53 Great Wood, Keswick
54 Falls of Clyde
55 Inverliever Forest
56 Glen More
57 Loch Garten

THE SOUTH WEST

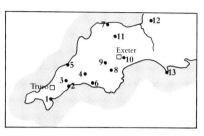

CORNWALL

1 Helford River

LOCATION **Access on foot at Mudgeon on the unclassified road from Mawgan to Manaccan. A vehicle track runs from the road to Tremayne Quay, but there are no parking facilities.** *Landranger Sheet 204, 728257.*

Of the scattered group of National Trust properties around the Helford River, Tremayne Woods on the south bank of the estuary hold the most interest for the bird-watcher. The very fact that this area is wooded is something of a rarity in west Cornwall – the presence of a varied bird population as well must be seen as an extra bonus. Situated on the steeply sloping sides of the river valley, Tremayne Woods comprise various strips of deciduous woodland, some of which (Great Wood and Little Wood) are extremely old. A good variety of tall canopy-forming trees – oak, beech ash and elm – with numerous smaller saplings and shrubs, makes for a structurally diverse habitat. Among the birds attracted to these woods are **tits, chaffinches, buzzards** and **nuthatches.** The Helford River is also of importance for wintering wildfowl and waders.

Highlights
Chiffchaff, great spotted woodpecker, nuthatch.

Time and season
Excellent all year, but if you have an interest in migrant waders, then the autumn-winter season can be rewarding. All year: **heron, mallard, buzzard, kestrel, pheasant, stock dove, great spotted woodpecker, jay, magpie, rook, carrion crow, wren, coal tit, blue tit, great tit, robin, mistle thrush, nuthatch, treecreeper, chaffinch, bullfinch.** Summer: **cuckoo, swallow, garden warbler, blackcap, whitethroat, wood warbler, willow warbler, chiffchaff.**

2 Fowey

LOCATION **On the east side of the estuary of the River Fowey, opposite the town of Fowey. Hall Walk and Pont Pill occupy the steeply sloping ground on either side of the Pont Pill creek. Follow the path that links the Polruan and Bodinnick ferries to Fowey.** *Landranger Sheet 200, 130520.*

A mosaic of woodland, scrub and bracken on the steep banks of the small creek of Pont Pill provides a favourable habitat for many small nesting birds. Hall Walk, on the northern side of the creek, boasts a well-developed scrub layer of blackthorn and hazel, which is being invaded by young saplings of syacamore and ash in the natural succession to woodland. In parts, much of this scrub layer is choked by a dense mat of Traveller's Joy, a creeper that is rarely found in any profusion in Cornwall. Fortunately for the **tits** and **finches** that breed here, the scrub is largely impenetrable beyond the path margins. Pont Pill, on the southern side, consists mainly of oak and hazel coppiced woodland. **Mallard** and **heron** may be observed on the mud-flats. Be on the look-out for **cirl bunting**, which used to breed in the area.

Highlights
Finches, tits, wrens.

Time and season
All year; but come early in the summer as this is a popular holiday area. All year: **heron, mallard, buzzard, woodpigeon, green woodpecker, jay, wren, coal tit, blue tit, great tit, robin, chaffinch, goldfinch, bullfinch.** Summer: **cuckoo, swallow, garden warbler, blackcap, whitethroat, willow warbler, chiffchaff.**

3 Lanhydrock

LOCATION **Two-and-a-half miles (4 km) south-east of Bodmin, off the B3268.** *Landranger Sheet 200, 085636.*

Situated in the valley of the River Fowey, Lanhydrock, with its splendid mature mixed woodlands, is probably the most important National Trust property in Cornwall for birds. Fortunately for the bird-watcher, most of the visitors do not venture far from Lanhydrock House, leaving areas such as Great Wood, on the southern side of the estate, relatively undisturbed. Here under the tall canopy dominated by oak and beech, you will have a chance of seeing **sparrowhawks, redstarts, wood warblers** and the **lesser spotted woodpecker** – the latter being a scarce breeding bird in Cornwall. Lanhydrock is also the only National Trust site in Cornwall where **pied flycatchers** have been recorded.

The house is a beautiful granite mansion dating from the 17th C.

Highlights
Pied flycatcher, siskin.

Time and season
Visit as early as possible in the morning, especially during the summer season when there is a large influx of tourists. An all-year route: look out for **warblers** in the summer and **siskin** in the winter. All year: **heron, sparrowhawk, wood-pigeon, green woodpecker, great spotted woodpecker, lesser spotted woodpecker, woodlark, grey wagtail, jay, rook, carrion crow, goldcrest, robin, blackbird, mistle thrush, song thrush, long-tailed tit, marsh tit, willow tit, coal tit, blue tit, great tit, nuthatch, treecreeper, chaffinch.** Summer migrants: **nightjar, swallow, house martin, blackcap, wood warbler, willow warbler, chiffchaff, pied flycatcher, spotted flycatcher, redstart.**

4 Cotehele

LOCATION **Fourteen miles (23 km) north of Plymouth, via the Saltash Bridge, Cotehele is situated on the west bank of the River Tamar, two miles (3 km) west of Calstock by footpath, or six miles (10 km) by road.** *Landranger Sheet 201, 420682.*

Dissected by three small tributaries of the River Tamar, the gently rounded hills of the Cotehele Estate offer a site of county importance for the diversity and quality of its breeding birds. Breeding species include **sparrowhawks** and **barn owls,** as well as **lesser spotted woodpeckers** and **garden** and **wood warblers** – all rare in Cornwall. Most of the property is intensively farmed, but there are, however, extensive areas of woodland on the steeper valley slopes. The most interesting of these is Cotehele Wood, a mature mixed deciduous woodland on the eastern side of the estate. The high, closed canopy with occasional large clearings provided by fallen trees is especially good for woodland birds. A pair of **woodlarks** are thought to breed somewhere on the estate – look out for them in the rough grassland areas near the woods.

Highlights
Barn owl, lesser spotted woodpecker, wood warbler.

Time and season
Thousands of visitors flock to Cotehele House each year, so come early. An all-year site: Cotehele is especially noted for the diversity of its wintering birds. All year: **buzzard, sparrowhawk, pheasant, stock dove, wood-pigeon, collared dove, barn owl, tawny owl, green woodpecker, great spotted woodpecker, lesser spotted woodpecker, woodlark,** pied wagtail, **grey wagtail, starling, magpie, jay, jackdaw, rook, carrion crow, wren, dunnock, goldcrest, long-tailed tit, marsh tit, coal tit, blue tit, great tit, robin, mistle thrush, nuthatch, treecreeper, chaffinch, greenfinch, goldfinch, bullfinch.** Summer: **swift, swallow, house martin, grasshopper warbler, sedge warbler, garden warbler, blackcap, whitethroat, wood warbler, willow warbler, chiffchaff, spotted flycatcher.**

5 Boscastle Harbour and Valency Valley

LOCATION **Three-and-a-half miles (5.5 km) north-east of Tintagel, on the B3263 road to Bude. There is a car park for about 150 cars in the village.** *Landranger Sheet 190, 0090 and 1191.*

Running from the harbour mouth to the village of Boscastle and then up the wooded valley to the east, this attractive National Trust property receives large numbers of visitors each day during the summer. Most visitors, however, keep to the coast, where from the flat-topped summit of Willapark Headland rising 300 ft (91 m) above sea level, fine sea views can be obtained. Guillemot and razorbills breed along the cliffs to the east of the harbour. The Valency Valley, by comparison, receives little disturbance, and it is in Peters Wood, on the north-facing slope, that you will spend a pleasurable day's birdwatching. The main part of the wood is oak-dominated, with sycamore, hazel and ash occurring more frequently near the river. **Goldcrest** are known to breed in this wood, and you are also likely to see **warblers, chiffchaffs** and **whitethroats** during the summer months. The River Valency itself is worthy of note – a clean, fast-flowing stream where you may catch a glimpse of the dipper as it bobs up and down in search of food. It can remain submerged for surprisingly long periods, and anchors itself to pebbles on the bottom.

Highlights
Buzzard, goldcrest.

Time and season
Early in the morning during the spring and summer months. All year: **heron, buzzard, kestrel, wood-pigeon, barn owl, magpie, jackdaw, rook, carrion crow, wren, dunnock, goldcrest, robin, coal tit, chaffinch.** Summer: **swallow, house martin, blackcap, whitethroat, willow warbler, chiffchaff.**

DEVON

6 Plym Bridge Woods

LOCATION Five miles (8 km) northeast of Plymouth. Turn off the A38 at Plympton and head north for three miles (5 km) in the direction of Plymouth Airport. *Landranger Sheet 201, 522595.*

Plym Bridge Woods occur at the confluence of the River Plym with a disused railway track and the remains of a former quarry, thus offering a wide variety of woodland habitats for birds, insects and small mammals. Old oak coppice predominates in Colwill Wood to the north of the property, but is replaced by mixed deciduous woodland on the valley slopes. Ash, sycamore and alder flourish in the wetter soils along the river bank, giving way to wych elm, hornbeam and hazel on the eastern side of the river. **Jays, treecreepers** and **spotted flycatchers** are just some of the birds you may see here, while along the sheltered corridor provided by the disused railway track, **tits, wrens** and **robins** flit among the gorse bushes.

Highlights
Lesser spotted woodpecker, sparrowhawk, tree pipit, wood warbler.

Time and season
Late spring and summer for visiting birds, although you will find this area interesting at any time. Try and catch the dawn chorus at first light. All year: **buzzard, sparrowhawk, lesser spotted woodpecker, grey wagtail, jay, wren, long-tailed tit, marsh tit, willow tit, coal tit, blue tit, great tit, robin, treecreeper.** Summer: **cuckoo, tree pipit, garden warbler, blackcap, wood warbler, willow warbler, chiffchaff, spotted flycatcher.**

---

7 Lynmouth

LOCATION The property lies to the east of Lynmouth, on both sides of the A39. Park your car at Barna Barrow, to the east of Countisbury village, for paths down to the river valleys. *Landranger Sheet 180, 7447.*

Lynmouth can be justly proud of its woodlands, for they represent one of the most extensive and structurally diverse sites owned by the National Trust in the whole of the country. Clothing the steeply sloping valleys of the East Lyn River and Hoar Oak Water, the woods exhibit an excellent variety of trees populated by a healthy community of breeding birds. Although many different tree stands occur on this property, the common pattern of distribution is to find oak coppice on the steep, well-drained slopes, and oak with various mixtures of ash, wych elm and alder in the valley bottoms. The river margins support the richest variety of birds, and breeding species include **pied flycatcher, redstart, wood warbler** and **sparrowhawk. Grey wagtails** and dippers are very much in evidence by the banks of the fast-flowing river, although their nests are heavily preyed upon by wild mink.

There are many signposted footpaths.

Highlights
Pied flycatcher, redstart.

Time and season
Spring and early summer if you want to catch the summer visitors in full song. All year: **heron, buzzard, sparrowhawk, kestrel, stock dove, wood-pigeon, tawny owl, green woodpecker, great spotted woodpecker,** meadow pipit, **grey**

wagtail, starling, magpie, jay, jack-daw, carrion crow, wren, dunnock, goldcrest, long-tailed tit, marsh tit, coal tit, blue tit, great tit, robin, mistle thrush, nuthatch, treecreeper, chaffinch, goldfinch, bullfinch. Summer: cuckoo, swallow, house martin, tree pipit, grasshopper warbler, garden warbler, blackcap, whitethroat, wood warbler, willow warbler, chiffchaff, pied flycatcher, spotted flycatcher, redstart.

8 Parke, Bovey Tracey

LOCATION Five miles (8 km) north-west of Newton Abbot, just outside the town of Bovey Tracey on the north side of the B3344 to Manaton. *Landranger Sheet 191, 805785.*

The wooded valley of the River Bovey forms one of the most beautiful approaches to Dartmoor, and is well worth a detour if you are in the area. The property itself consists largely of woodland and wet meadows, with a section of disused railway track running roughly parallel to the northern side of the river. The scrubby embankments of the railway track provide good cover for **bullfinches,** although the most interesting variety of birds inhabits Blackmoor Copse, in the northern part of the estate, and Bearacleave Wood, a patch of oakwood rising steeply out of the valley to the north-east. Developed over the alluvial river flats, Blackmoor Copse is an old coppiced woodland consisting mainly of alder, ash and oak with a healthy shrub layer. **Heron** and

grey wagtails are often espied along the river bank.

Highlights
Buzzard, grey wagtail.

Time and season
All year; although come early during the summer months to avoid the holiday-makers. All year: **heron, buzzard, wood-pigeon, grey wagtail, magpie, rook, wren, coal tit, blue tit, great tit, robin, nuthatch, treecreeper, bullfinch.** Summer: **turtle dove, cuckoo, garden warbler, blackcap, willow warbler.**

9 Castle Drogo

LOCATION At Drewsteignton, four miles (6.5 km) north-east of Chag-ford. Turn off the A382 at Sandy Park. *Landranger 191, 723902.*

Castle Drogo offers a rich and varied habitat of coppiced oak woodland, heath and grassland. Flowing through the central part of the Estate is the River Teign, a shallow, stony-bottomed river favoured by **grey wagtails**. Bordering the southern side of the river for part of its course are the boulder-strewn oak coppices of Whiddon Wood which are rich in mosses and ferns near the water's edge. Whiddon Wood, like Drewston Wood to the east, holds a thriving community of woodland birds, including **nuthatches, tits, jays** and **woodpeckers**. North of the river, where the trees give way to the open heath of Piddledown Common, **wrens** and **whitethroats** can be found amongst

the bracken and gorse, while **buzzards** and **kestrels** are often seen overhead.

Highlights
Grey wagtail, nuthatch.

Time and season
All year, but summer is the most popular time. All year: **buzzard, kestrel, wood-pigeon, green woodpecker, grey wagtail, magpie, jay, wren, marsh tit, coal tit, blue tit, great tit, robin, nuthatch, chaffinch.** Summer: **swallow, blackcap, whitethroat, wood warbler, willow warbler, chiffchaff, redstart.**

10 Killerton

LOCATION Seven miles (11 km) north-east of Exeter, on either side of the Exeter-Cullompton road (B3181). *Landranger Sheet 192, 9897.*

A bird-watcher's haven, this: not only is there a wide range of wetland and woodland habitats, but two areas within the property (Killerton Park and Ashclyst Forest) have been identified by the British Trust for Ornithology as sites of local importance for breeding and wintering birds. Two rivers, the Clyst and the Culm, meander through the estate, one of which (the River Culm) is a wide, slow-moving affair with well-developed aquatic vegetation. **Moorhen** and **mallard** are frequently seen here. But by far the most interesting areas are Ashclyst Forest, situated on high ground to the east, and Poundapit, Welspring and Oakham Copses to the north-east.

These woods are noted for their thriving bird populations, and you should seek out the small stream valleys with mature stands of oak and ash, interspersed with holly and hazel in the shrub layer. Ashclyst Forest in particular features a large variety of deciduous trees of different ages and densities, providing a rich habitat overall for birds and insects. Breeding birds include **buzzard, sparrowhawk, redstart** and **wood warbler,** to name but a few. Killerton Park woodlands, to the north-west of the property, is also worth a visit if you have time. The wooded clump known as Dolbury used to be the site of a **heronry,** and there have been recent schemes to encourage its re-establishment.

Highlights
Buzzard, lesser spotted wood-pecker, sparrowhawk.

Time and season
Excellent all year, but avoid those days booked for public events (caravan rallies and the like). Look out for **warblers** in the summer, and **redwings** and **siskins** in the winter. All year: **heron, buzzard, mallard, sparrowhawk, kestrel, pheasant, moorhen, wood-cock, stock dove, wood-pigeon, collared dove, barn owl, little owl, tawny owl, green woodpecker, great spotted woodpecker, lesser spotted woodpecker,** meadow pipit, **grey wagtail, starling, magpie, jay, jackdaw, rook, carrion crow, wren, dunnock, goldcrest, long-tailed tit, marsh tit, coal tit, blue tit, great tit, nuthatch, robin, mistle thrush, treecreeper, chaffinch, greenfinch,**

bullfinch, goldfinch, cirl bunting. Summer: **turtle dove, cuckoo, night-jar, swallow, house martin, tree pipit, grasshopper warbler, sedge warbler, garden warbler, blackcap, whitethroat, lesser whitethroat, wood warbler, willow warbler, chiffchaff, pied flycatcher, spotted flycatcher, crossbill, hawfinch.** Winter: **firecrest, fieldfare, redwing, brambling, siskin, redpoll.**

SOMERSET

11 Barle Valley

LOCATION **Four miles (6.5 km) north-west of Dulverton, off the B3223. Follow signs for Hawkridge. Landranger Sheet 181, 870291.**

Mature oak and beech trees predominate in this charming wooded valley – a sight once common throughout the West Country before the introduction of fast-growing conifers. These mixed woodlands support a rich and varied bird population, and you will see **warblers, redstarts** and **flycatchers** in abundance. The open scrub and bracken slopes harbour **tree pipits, cuckoos** and yellowhammers, while on East Anstey Common you are quite likely to see stonechats, whinchats and linnets. **Kestrels** are commonly seen hovering in this area, and in the winter, the occasional merlin may be spotted, darting close to the ground.

Highlights
Wood warblers, redstarts and the patchily distributed **pied flycatcher.**

Time and season
April-June. Come early in the morning if you want to see the birds during their active period. All year: **buzzard, sparrowhawk, kestrel, green wood-pecker, great spotted woodpecker, lesser spotted woodpecker, grey wagtail, nuthatch.** Summer migrants: **cuckoo, tree pipit, wood warbler, willow warbler, chiffchaff, pied flycatcher, spotted flycatcher, redstart.**

---

12 Cheddar Cliffs

LOCATION **Eight miles (13 km) north-west of Wells. Landranger Sheet 182, 468543.**

To a bird-watcher, the spectacular scenery at Cheddar immediately suggests crag-nesting birds. Indeed, ravens and **buzzards** are among the species to be seen hovering over the deep Gorge, or perched on limestone ledges high above the road. However, there are large areas of scrub and grassland on the flat plateau through which the Gorge runs, and here many small seed- and insect-eating birds breed, and visitors find food and shelter. Much of the Gorge is woodland, too, which of course provides further roosts and nesting sites.

Highlights
Birds of prey hunting above the gorge.

Time and season
Most interesting in the spring and summer, but avoid holiday periods when the Gorge is choked with visitors. All year: **buzzard, kestrel, wood-**

pigeon, **magpie, jackdaw, rook, carrion crow, jay, song thrush, blackbird, robin, goldcrest, goldfinch, bullfinch, chaffinch.** Spring and summer: **swift, blackcap, whitethroat, lesser whitethroat, willow warbler, chiffchaff.**

DORSET

13 Portland Bill

LOCATION **Head south from Weymouth on the A354, following signs for Portland. There is a car park at the tip of the Bill just north of the new lighthouse.** *Landranger Sheet 194, 677686.*

This must surely be one of the prime spots in England for observing migrants of all types. Jutting six miles (10 km) out into the English Channel, this windswept promontory of small stone-walled fields and thorny hedges is a regular staging post for chats, **warblers** and **flycatchers,** not to mention the rarer passerines (including melodious, icterine and sub-Alpine warblers, ortolan bunting and tawny pipit) which can and do turn up with surprising frequency. The Portland Bird Observatory is located here; ringing and netting are carried out annually and a log recording recent sightings is available on request. Besides being a marvellous location for observing migrating passerines, Portland Bill also offers excellent views of sea-birds not normally seen close to the shore. Manx and Balearic shearwaters are regular species, and puffins breed on the western cliffs.

Highlights

So many rarities turn up that it is difficult to single out two or three species; however, look out for **pied flycatchers,** melodious and icterine warblers, ortolan buntings and tawny pipits.

Time and season

The migration months of March-May and August-October are the best times to visit, although a fascinating variety of birds can be seen at any time of year. All year: **sparrowhawk, kestrel, little owl, goldfinch,** Dartford warbler, corn bunting. Summer migrants: **cuckoo, tree pipit, grasshopper warbler, sedge warbler, garden warbler, pied flycatcher, spotted flycatcher.**

THE SOUTH EAST

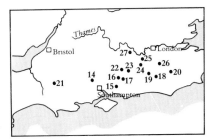

HAMPSHIRE

14 Mottisfont Abbey

LOCATION **About 12 miles (20 km) north-west of Southampton, just off the B3084 at Lockerley.** *Landranger Sheet 185, 327270.*

A beautiful 12th-C abbey lies at the heart of this well-wooded estate. The River Test meanders across the eastern edge of the estate, but the main interest from the point of view of birdlife lies in the many areas of ancient oak, ash and hazel woodland scattered throughout the west and north. Beneath their spreading canopy there is plenty of shrubbery and ground cover which harbours a rich variety of insects and birds including all three species of **woodpecker.** Passage migrants also take refuge here in good numbers, and there are recent records of **nightingales.** The woods are managed for shooting, so access may be limited, but observation at least of the margins and of the many coppices is usually unrestricted.

Highlights

Excellent variety of **tits, thrushes** and **warblers,** many breeding birds.

Time and season

Visit in the early summer when bird-song is at its peak. All year: **heron, mallard, buzzard, pheasant, wood-cock, stock dove, wood-pigeon, barn owl, little owl, swift, green, great** and **lesser spotted wood-peckers, magpie, jay, jackdaw, rook, carrion crow, goldcrest, mistle thrush, song thrush, great, blue, coal** and **long-tailed tits, nuthatch, chaffinch, greenfinch, redpoll, bullfinch, reed bunting.** Spring and summer: **turtle dove, cuckoo, swallow, house martin, sedge, garden** and **willow warblers, blackcap, whitethroat** and **lesser whitethroat, chiffchaff, spotted flycatcher, goldfinch.**

15 Queen Elizabeth Country Park

LOCATION Proceed north from Portsmouth on the A3 through Horndean. Three miles (5 km) beyond Horndean you will see signs for the Queen Elizabeth Country Park. Base yourself at the car park there. *Landranger Sheet 197, 718182; admission fee.*

The Nature Trails skirt around a variety of habitats, from well-established mixed woodland in the Queen Elizabeth Forest, to open scrub and downland on Butser Hill. Farmland birds abound on the edge of the Park,

while in the woodland itself, a thriving population of **warblers, turtle doves, tits** and **woodpeckers** can be found. On the downland, meadow pipits, skylarks and **green woodpeckers** feed out in the open, and **sparrowhawks** are frequently seen soaring overhead. While in the woods, look out for the recently introduced golden pheasant feeding under the conifers.

Highlights

Warblers and **woodpeckers.**

Time and season

All year, although early mornings in spring are particularly interesting in the wooded areas. All year: **sparrowhawk, kestrel, black-headed gull, great spotted woodpecker,** skylark, meadow pipit, **magpie, jackdaw, rook, carrion crow, willow tit, chaffinch, greenfinch.** Summer: **turtle dove, grasshopper warbler, sedge warbler, garden warbler, blackcap, lesser whitethroat, wood warbler, willow warbler.**

16 Selborne Hill

LOCATION Off the B3006 some 4 miles (6 km) south of Alton. *Land-ranger Sheet 186, 735333.*

The 18th-C naturalist Gilbert White made this area famous when he published the results of a detailed study in *The Natural History of Selborne.* Today, the mature broad-leaved woods are as popular with knowledgeable naturalists following White's footsteps as they are with local people enjoying a walk in the

shade, or on the chalky grassland at the summit. The hill is at the western end of the Weald, and slopes steeply away at the north-east and north-west; the slopes are gentler on other sides. Most of the woodland is beech, but there are also many ash, field maple, hazel and yew trees. Birdlife is rich and varied, with most of the species typical of broad-leaved woodland present.

In the main street of Selborne village is a useful bookshop specializing in natural history and countryside publications; you can also visit *The Wakes,* home of Gilbert White.

Highlights

The shy **hawfinch** is to be found high up among the beeches at Selborne Hanger; listen for its sharp 'tick' call.

Time and season

The sharp-eyed may see **owls** at dusk. Spring and summer will provide the best variety of species. All year: **kestrel, pheasant, moorhen, woodcock, stock dove, wood-pigeon, little owl, tawny owl, green, great** and **lesser spotted woodpeckers, carrion crow, rook, jackdaw, magpie, jay, goldcrest, mistle thrush, song thrush, great, blue, coal, marsh** and **long-tailed tits, nuthatch, tree-creeper, wren, mistle thrush, song thrush, robin, tree sparrow, chaffinch, greenfinch, redpoll, bull-finch, hawfinch.** Winter: **brambling, fieldfare.** Spring and summer: **turtle dove, cuckoo, swift, swallow, house martin, grasshopper, garden** and **willow warblers, blackcap, nightin-gale, whitethroat, chiffchaff, spot-ted flycatcher, goldfinch.**

WEST SUSSEX

17 Durford Heath

LOCATION **Two-and-a-half miles (4 km) north-east of Petersfield, on the Rogate to Liss road.** *Landranger Sheet 197, 788256.*

In this small, gently-rolling estate there is a widely varied bird population, though no one species is particularly numerous. The woodland is about half oak, and half Scots Pine – despite the name, there are only small areas of heath. Of the birds that nest in the tall trees, most are **doves, tits** and **warblers.**

Highlights
Tawny owls hunting at dusk.

Time and season
Visit during the breeding season. All year: **sparrowhawk, pheasant, stock dove, wood-pigeon, green** and **great spotted woodpeckers, magpie, jay, carrion crow, great, blue, coal, marsh** and **long-tailed tit, nuthatch, treecreeper, wren, mistle** and **song thrushes, blackbird, robin, goldcrest, greenfinch, chaffinch.** Spring and summer: **turtle dove, willow warbler, chiffchaff, tree pipit.**

18 Wakehurst Place

LOCATION **One mile (1.5 km) north of Ardingly village on the B2028 Turners Hill road.** *Landranger Sheet 187, 339314.*

Wakehurst Place is administered as an outstation by The Royal Botanic Gardens, Kew. The gardens are open to the public from 10.00 am until an hour before dusk, and there is a £1.50 entrance fee. Deep valleys and outcrops of sandstone carve across the Estate, and to add further variety to the landscape and birdlife, there are a lake and large areas of woodland. Tilgate, Horsebridge and West Woods have the greatest variety of birds, with nearly 50 species breeding; **tits** and **finches** are particularly well represented. The lawns around the house (which is not open to the public) attract **green woodpecker, jackdaw,** and **starling** from a large colony in West Wood.

Highlights
An unusually larger variety of small birds breeding.

Time and season
Best in spring and summer months. All year: **mallard, Canada goose, sparrowhawk, kestrel, pheasant, moorhen, woodcock, stock dove, wood-pigeon, tawny owl, green, great** and **lesser spotted woodpecker, magpie, jay, jackdaw, carrion crow, great, blue, coal, marsh, willow** and **long-tailed tits, treecreeper, wren, mistle** and **song thrushes, blackbird, robin, goldcrest, grey wagtail, starling, hawfinch, greenfinch, goldfinch, redpoll, bullfinch, chaffinch, reed bunting, house sparrow, tree sparrow.** Spring and summer: **turtle dove, cuckoo, garden** and **willow warblers, blackcap, chiffchaff, spotted flycatcher.**

19 Nymans Gardens

LOCATION **Four-and-a-half miles (3 km) south of Crawley, just off the London to Brighton (A23) road.** *Landranger Sheet 187, 265294.*

The formal gardens at Nymans are justly famous, but visitors who are interested in the birdlife of the area would be well advised to leave the gardens themselves, and walk around the surrounding parkland. Much of this large estate is covered in mature broad-leaved woodland, and from a scientific point of view the woods are among the best in Sussex. Many species of birds build their nests in the oak, ash, hazel and beech trees, and though the woodland structure favours small birds such as **warblers, tits** and **finches,** there are larger birds, too, including **owls** and birds of prey. Lengths of hedgerow – an important bird habitat that continues to decline on a national scale – add to the number of species that can be seen here. The most interesting and varied of the woods on the estate is Cow Wood, which is crossed by numerous paths.

Highlights
All three species of **woodpecker** breed here.

Time and season
Visit in spring or early summer to see the greatest abundance of birds. All year: **Heron, sparrowhawk, pheasant, moorhen, woodcock, stock dove, collared dove, wood-pigeon, tawny owl, green, great** and **lesser spotted woodpeckers, carrion crow, jack-**

daw, magpie, jay, goldcrest, mistle thrush, song thrush, great, blue, coal, marsh, willow and long-tailed tits, nuthatch, treecreeper, wren, robin, chaffinch, greenfinch, bullfinch, hawfinch. Winter: brambling. Spring and summer: cuckoo, garden, wood and willow warblers, blackcap, whitethroat, chiffchaff, goldfinch.

EAST SUSSEX

20 Nap Wood

LOCATION Four miles (7 km) south of Tunbridge Wells on the A267. *Landranger Sheet 188, 585330.*

Mature oak trees line the steep-sided stream valleys at Nap Wood Nature Reserve in the Central Weald, protecting the flora and fauna beneath from extremes of climate, and providing a feast of acorns for the numerous wood-pigeons high in the canopy. There is also alder woodland, which supports a rich insect population and a variety of tits. Other species of birds typical of oak woodlands can also be seen here.

Highlights
Breeding population of wood warbler.

Time and season
The circular path through the Reserve is open only on Sundays between April and October, and at other times by permit; write to The Sussex Trust for Nature Conservation, Woods Mill, Henfield,

Sussex. All year: sparrowhawk, kestrel, woodcock, stock dove, wood-pigeon, tawny owl, great spotted woodpecker, magpie, jay, rook, carrion crow, great, blue, coal and long-tailed tits, treecreeper, wren, mistle and song thrushes, blackbird, robin, starling, greenfinch, goldfinch, redpoll, bullfinch, chaffinch, reed bunting, house sparrow, tree sparrow. Spring and summer: cuckoo, swift, swallow, house martin, redstart, grasshopper, garden, willow and wood warblers, blackcap, whitethroat, chiffchaff, tree pipit.

WILTSHIRE

21 Stourhead

LOCATION At Stourton, off the B3092, 3 miles (2 km) north-west of Mere. *Landranger Sheet 183, 770350.*

Stourhead lies in picturesque, gently-rolling countryside, and the landscape gardeners who transfigured the area in the mid-18th C made full use of the springs to form a series of ornamental lakes. These are now the home of breeding water-birds. The landscaping process also replaced many native British species of tree and plant with introduced and ornamental varieties. However, some of the original ancient woodland remains today, and these areas contribute heavily to the variety of birdlife that can be seen here. Look also at the hedgerows – where they have not been too heavily trimmed.

Highlights
Large variety of breeding birds.

Time and season
Most interesting in the spring and early summer, though some water birds overwinter on the lakes. All year: mallard, buzzard, kestrel, pheasant, moorhen, woodcock, stock dove, wood-pigeon, collared dove, tawny owl, great spotted and green woodpeckers, carrion crow, jackdaw, magpie, jay, great, blue, long-tailed and coal tits, nuthatch, treecreeper, wren, mistle and song thrushes, blackbird, robin, goldcrest, pied and grey wagtails, greenfinch, bullfinch, chaffinch, goldfinch. Spring and summer: cuckoo, swift, swallow, house martin, rook, blackcap, garden and willow warblers.

SURREY

22 Alice Holt Forest

LOCATION Three miles (5 km) south-west of Farnham, off the A325. Turn left at Bucks Horn Oak on to the Batt's Corner road and follow signs for the Visitor Centre and car park. *Landranger Sheet 186, 813413.*

Although Alice Holt Forest now belongs to the Forestry Commission, it used to be part of an extensive royal hunting ground. Some deciduous and coniferous trees date back to the early-19th C, and attract a pleasing variety of **warblers, woodpeckers** and **flycatchers.**

Highlights
Lesser spotted woodpecker, spotted flycatcher, willow warbler.

Time and season
All year, although April-June is probably the best time. Visit early in the morning, when the woodland birds are most active. All year: **kestrel, great spotted woodpecker, lesser spotted woodpecker, goldcrest, long-tailed tit, coal tit, nuthatch, treecreeper, redpoll.** Summer: **garden warbler, blackcap, willow warbler, chiffchaff, spotted flycatcher.** Winter: **siskin.**

23 Hindhead

LOCATION **Twelve miles (20 km) south-west of Guildford, on both sides of the A3 to Portsmouth.** *Landranger Sheet 186, 930360.*

The National Trust owns numerous pockets of land in this area, but by far the largest continuous property is Hindhead Common, Inval and Hurt Hills. This 1,000 acre area encompasses both steep slopes and gently rolling scenery, and is covered by an intricate mosaic of woodland, scrub, heath and bracken. Of these habitats, the mature broad-leaved woods and heath have the richest bird populations. Look especially for birch and alder woodland, and pay particular attention to scattered trees and saplings on the small open areas of heath. Walking through stands of bracken

along the paths may flush out some small birds, too, without risk of disturbance to nesting birds.

Highlights
There have been occasional sightings of the rare Dartford warbler here, and birds of prey can often be seen passing or overwintering.

Time and season
Worth a visit at any time of year, but best when birds are breeding. All year: **mallard, sparrowhawk, kestrel, pheasant, woodcock, stock dove, wood-pigeon, green** and **great spotted woodpeckers, magpie, jay, jackdaw, rook, carrion crow, great, blue, coal, marsh** and **long-tailed tits, treecreeper, wren, mistle** and **song thrushes, blackbird, robin, goldcrest, starling, greenfinch, goldfinch, bullfinch, chaffinch, reed bunting, house sparrow, tree sparrow.** Winter: **redpoll, fieldfare.** Spring and summer: **turtle dove, cuckoo, nightjar, woodlark, swift, swallow, redstart, nightingale, grasshopper, garden, willow** and **wood warblers, blackcap, whitethroat** and **lesser whitethroat, chiffchaff, tree pipit.**

24 Holmwood Common

LOCATION **About a mile (1.5 km) south of Dorking, mostly east of the A24 road to Horsham.** *Landranger Sheet 187, 170460.*

Dense scrub and thickets of young oak and birch trees cover much of

the Common, and in these areas it is hard to get a good view of what birdlife there is. The most promising areas are in the south, where the trees are older and there is more open space. It is less muddy here, too. Throughout the Common, clearings and wide paths are probably the best places to observe birds.

Highlights
Good chance of seeing **great spotted woodpecker.**

Time and season
Most of the smaller birds are here throughout the year, though birdlife is generally more conspicuous in spring and summer. All year: **heron, mallard, Canada goose, kestrel, moorhen, wood-pigeon, great spotted woodpecker, magpie, jay, great, blue, marsh** and **long-tailed tits, treecreeper, wren, song thrush, blackbird, robin, starling, bullfinch, chaffinch.** Spring/summer: **swallow, cuckoo, willow warbler, chiffchaff, garden warbler, blackcap.**

25 Box Hill

LOCATION **One mile (1.5 km) north of Dorking, east of the A24.** *Landranger Sheet 187, 170510.*

Box Hill is part of the North Downs ridge, but actually appears to rise quite separate and distinct from the surrounding countryside. It is a steep-sided escarpment, cut away on the west by the River Mole. Much of the hill is wooded, not just by box, but also by a diversity of other broad-leaved trees.

The best spots to observe the birdlife are at the edge of the River Mole where it meanders along a flat plateau at the foot of the hill. Here it is possible to see a good variety of woodland and water-birds, including the occasional king-fisher. Nearby scrub and grassland adds to the diversity of available bird habitats.

All in all the Trust owns or protects more than 1,000 acres in the vicinity. The North Downs Way borders and traverses the property.

Highlights
Possibility of seeing a tremendous variety of small birds.

Time and season
Always some activity, but like any wooded area, most interesting during the breeding season. All year: **heron, mallard, sparrowhawk, kestrel, pheasant, moorhen, woodcock, stock dove, wood-pigeon, collared dove, little owl, tawny owl, green, great** and **lesser spotted wood-peckers, magpie, jay, jackdaw, rook, carrion crow, great, blue, coal, marsh** and **long-tailed tits, nuthatch, treecreeper, wren, mistle** and **song thrushes, blackbird, robin, goldcrest, grey wagtail, hawfinch, greenfinch, chaffinch, bullfinch, reed bunting, tree sparrow.** Winter: **redwing, fieldfare.** Spring and sum-mer: **turtle dove, swift, green wood-pecker, swallow, house martin, redstart, nightingale, sedge warbler, blackcap, grasshopper, garden, willow** and **wood warblers, whitethroat, lesser whitethroat, chiffchaff, pied** and **spotted flycat-chers, tree pipit.**

26 Limpsfield Common and The Chart

LOCATION **South of the A25 linking Oxted and Westerham, on the Kent border.** *Landranger Sheet 187, 410525.*

Broad-leaved woodland dominates the scenery at this point on the gently-sloping sandy ground between North and South Downs. The trees are mostly oak, birch and sycamore, and there are some areas of pine and beech. Addi-tionally, there is some open grassland and heath. Birdlife is much in evidence in the woods; even after sunset you may hear **nightjar**, **owls** and **nightingale**, and on spring mornings the woods are alive with birdsong. In winter the mild southern climate and protected position makes this an important overwintering area for **thrushes** and **finches.**

Highlights
Large numbers and variety of small birds – 66 species are recorded as breeding here.

Time and season
Good throughout the year. All year: **heron, mallard, sparrowhawk, kestrel, pheasant, moorhen, wood-cock, black-headed gull, stock dove, wood-pigeon, collared dove, little owl, tawny owl, green, great** and **lesser spotted woodpecker, magpie, jay, jackdaw, rook, carrion crow, great, blue, coal, marsh, willow** and **long-tailed tits, treecreeper, wren, mistle** and **song thrushes, blackbird, robin, goldcrest, grey wagtail, star-ling, hawfinch, greenfinch, gold-**

finch, bullfinch, crossbill, chaf-finch, reed bunting, house sparrow, tree sparrow.** Winter: **siskin, red-poll, fieldfare, redwing.** Spring and summer: **turtle dove, cuckoo, night-jar, woodlark, swift, swallow, house martin, redstart, nightingale, grass-hopper, garden, willow** and **wood warblers, blackcap, whitethroat** and **lesser whitethroat, chiffchaff, spot-ted flycatcher, tree pipit.**

27 Virginia Water

LOCATION **The lake lies two-and-a-half miles (4 km) south-west of Egham, almost opposite the junc-tion of the A30 with the B389.** *Land-ranger Sheet 175, 980688.*

For an area close to London and yet rich in birdlife, Virginia Water is hard to beat. Flanking the lake are old mixed woodlands, scrub and parkland, which hold a variety of birds, notably **tits, finches, woodpeckers** and **warblers.** The lake itself is worth a visit just to catch sight of the mandarin duck – a recently introduced species.

Highlights
Hawfinch, great spotted wood-pecker, lesser spotted woodpecker, siskin, warblers, woodcock.

Time and season
All year; although the widest variety of birds may be seen during spring and early summer. All year: **mallard, spar-rowhawk, kestrel, woodcock, green woodpecker, great spotted wood-pecker, lesser spotted woodpecker,**

grey wagtail, goldcrest, long-tailed tit, marsh tit, coal tit, blue tit, great tit, song thrush, mistle thrush, nuthatch, treecreeper, redpoll, crossbill, hawfinch. Summer migrants: sedge warbler, garden warbler, blackcap, willow warbler.

WALES

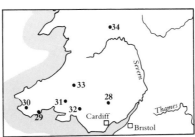

GWENT

28 Sugar Loaf

LOCATION **One-and-a-half miles (2 km) north-west of Abergavenny.** *Landranger Sheet 161, 268167.*

Sugar Loaf is a prominent and famous local mountain, rising to nearly 2,000 ft (610 m) above sea level. There is oak woodland covering much of the area, and heather or bracken blankets most of the remainder. Woodland birds are best seen in the steep-sloping wood known as St Mary's Vale (275170); 28 species are known to breed here, and there is a Nature Trail through the wood. Out of the woods, there are good bird populations too, both in the heather and in the bracken. Around the summit, listen for the song of the ring ouzel in summer. Stream valleys on the mountain are good for birds particularly in marshy areas, where wetland species can often be seen.

Highlights
Wood warbler and **redstart.**

Time and season
Something of interest at most times of the year. All year: **sparrowhawk, buzzard, kestrel, pheasant, stock dove, wood-pigeon, little owl, tawny owl, green** and **great spotted woodpeckers, magpie, jay, jackdaw, carrion crow, great, blue, coal, marsh** and **long-tailed tits, nuthatch, treecreeper, wren, mistle** and **song thrushes, blackbird, robin, goldcrest, starling, greenfinch, goldfinch, bullfinch, chaffinch, house sparrow, tree sparrow.** Winter: **fieldfare, redwing, siskin, waxwing.** Spring and summer: **heron, mallard, woodcock, rook, cuckoo, nightjar, swift, swallow, house martin, redstart, lesser spotted woodpecker, grasshopper, garden, willow** and **wood warblers, blackcap, whitethroat, chiffchaff, spotted** and **pied flycatchers, grey wagtail, tree pipit.**

DYFED

29 Colby Estate

LOCATION **Stretching inland from Carmarthen Bay at Amroth.** *Landranger Sheet 158, 155080.*

Most of the estate is arable and pasture land, which is of no particular bird interest. However, the rounded hills in this area are divided by steep-sided wooded valleys, where birdlife is much more interesting. Small birds nest in the valleys and in occasional thickets of trees and feed on the abundant insect population both in wooded areas and in scrubland. The most interesting woodland area lies to the left of the path leading towards the coast from Colby Lodge; pay attention to hedgerows, too, particularly in the western part of the estate. The coastline here is not particularly good for sea-birds, but there may be land-birds in the scrub that grows on the undercliff.

Highlights
Good range of **tits** and **warblers**.

Time and season
Best during summer and spring. All year: **heron, wood-pigeon, green woodpecker, great spotted wood-pecker, jackdaw, magpie, jay, great, blue** and **coal tits, treecreeper, wren, blackbird, robin, chaffinch.** Spring and summer: **garden** and **willow warblers, whitethroat, chiff-chaff.**

30 Little Milford

LOCATION **Three miles (5 km) south of Haverfordwest, on the Western Cleddau.** *Landranger Sheets 158 and 157, 967118.*

The Little Milford Estate consists of low-lying land overlooking a branch of the Daugleddau Estuary. The best population of woodland birds is to be found in the three stands of ancient oak woods scattered around the area. Adjacent conifer plantations are of little interest to bird-watchers. A further area of interest is the salt-marsh at the water's edge: this provides food for wildfowl, including large numbers of

wigeon, pintail, goldeneye, shoveler and shelduck, which overwinter in the estuary.

Highlights
Buzzards often visible hunting overhead.

Time and season
Spring/summer for breeding birds; wildfowl interest in winter. All year: **buzzard, wood-pigeon, magpie, great, coal** and **long-tailed tits, wren, robin, chaffinch.** Spring and summer: **willow** and **wood warblers, chiffchaff.**

31 Castle Woods

LOCATION **Head for Llandeilo on the A483 from Ammanford, or on the A40 from Carmarthen. Castle Woods is situated at the base of the ruins of Dynevor Castle, to the west of Llandeilo.** *Landranger Sheet 159, 627225.*

Although the castle itself is not open to the public, the nearby woods, which are owned by the West Wales Naturalists' Trust, offer a fine day's outing to the keen bird-watcher. The range of woodland birds includes **wood-peckers, tits, flycatchers** and **warblers.** Visitors are requested to keep to the paths, and to follow the fence lines when crossing fields in order to minimize disturbance.

Highlights
Buzzard, lesser spotted wood-pecker, pied flycatcher.

Time and season
April-June is the best time, if you want to see the full range of summer migrants. All year: **buzzard, sparrow-hawk, kestrel, green woodpecker, great spotted woodpecker, lesser spotted woodpecker, jay, goldcrest, long-tailed tit, marsh tit, willow tit, coal tit, nuthatch, treecreeper.** Summer: **garden warbler, blackcap, whitethroat, wood warbler, chiff-chaff, pied flycatcher, redstart.**

32 Dinas Hill, Gwenffrwd

LOCATION **Head from Llandovery towards Rhandirmwyn on unclassi-fied roads. Dinas Hill lies to the left of the road between Rhandirmwyn and the Llyn Brianne Reservoir. There is a car park at Nant-y-ffin, just past the church of St Paulinus.** *Landranger Sheet 147, 788471.*

Stunning landscapes of deep river valleys and rugged hillsides provide a marvellous backdrop for the numerous breeding birds you can see here. Follow the RSPB Nature Trail that starts alongside a small stream and finally encircles Dinas Hill. **Herons** are often seen near the water, while the wood holds an abundance of **tits, warblers** and **nuthatches. Buzzards,** ravens and **kestrels** soar over the craggy hillside – you may even catch a glimpse of the red kite, for which Dinas Hill once provided a famous nesting site.

Highlights
Grey wagtail, stock dove, tree pipit.

Time and season

Summer is the best time of year; come early if you want to avoid the large numbers of visitors. All year: **heron, buzzard, kestrel, stock dove, grey wagtail, jay, long-tailed tit, willow tit, coal tit, blue tit, great tit, nuthatch, treecreeper.** Summer migrants: **tree pipit, wood warbler, willow warbler, pied flycatcher, redstart.**

POWYS

33 Henrhyd Falls and Craigllech Woods

LOCATION **Eleven miles (17.5 km) north of Neath, between the A4067 and A4109 roads.** *Landranger Sheet 160, 850119.*

At Henrhyd Falls, the Nant Rhyd flows through a narrow wooded gorge with lush mossy sides. To the west of the falls there is another substantial wood, and the whole area has a thriving bird community. The mix of woodland species is broadest north of the river. South-east of Coelbren village there is wet grassland, where it may occasionally be possible to see waders feeding.

Highlights

Flycatchers acrobatically chasing insects near the falls.

Time and season

Good all year, but best in the summer. All year: **wood-pigeon, tawny owl, green** and **great spotted wood-** peckers, **carrion crow, magpie, great, marsh** and **long-tailed tits, nuthatch, treecreeper, wren, robin,** pied and **grey wagtails, starling, bullfinch, chaffinch, reed bunting.** Spring and summer: curlew, **swift, swallow, house martin,** dipper, **redstart, chiffchaff, wood warbler, pied flycatcher.**

CLWYD

34 Erddig

LOCATION **Two miles (3 km) south of Wrexham, off the A525.** *Landranger Sheet 118, 326482.*

The interest of Erddig does not end with the agricultural museum and the 17th-C house and gardens: within the extensive agricultural estate that surrounds them are several areas of woodland which are rich in birdlife, and a long stretch of the River Clywedog. Though polluted by coal dust, the river still manages to support kingfisher and dipper, and other water-birds. The most interesting areas of woodland are Hafod Wood, which is a Nature Reserve maintained by the North Wales Naturalists' Trust, and Big Wood. Both have good numbers of breeding birds. There are in addition areas of wet grassland, and some 70 small ponds; and the insects that breed in the ponds form a valuable food source for insect-eating birds from the nearby woods.

Highlights

Breeding birds – 49 species in Big Wood alone.

Time and season

Best in spring, but some birdlife including **finches, thrushes** and **tits** throughout the year. All year: **heron, mallard, buzzard, sparrowhawk, kestrel, pheasant, moorhen, woodcock, stock dove, wood-pigeon, barn owl, little owl, tawny owl, green, great** and **lesser spotted woodpecker, magpie, jay, jackdaw, rook, carrion crow, great, blue, coal, marsh** and **long-tailed tits, treecreeper, wren, mistle** and **song thrushes, blackbird, robin, goldcrest, grey wagtail, starling, greenfinch, goldfinch, bullfinch, house sparrow, tree sparrow.** Winter: **fieldfare, redwing, siskin.** Spring and summer: **turtle dove, cuckoo, swift, swallow, redstart, grasshopper, garden** and **willow warblers, blackcap, whitethroat, chiffchaff, spotted flycatcher.**

MIDDLE ENGLAND

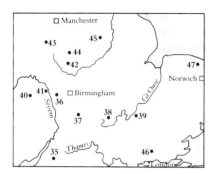

GLOUCESTERSHIRE

35 Newark Park

LOCATION **One-and-a-half miles (2 km) east of Wotton-under-Edge.** *Landranger Sheet 172, 786934.*

There are good views of the River Severn from the summit of this spur of the Cotswolds, and on the steep climb to the top there is plenty to see in the way of birdlife. The area is a mixture of farmland and ancient ash-oak woodlands; all the woods have a varied bird population, but Lower Lodge Wood is particularly good, and is managed as a Nature Reserve for this reason. In all, 29 species of birds breed in Newark Park.

Highlights
Good numbers of **tits** and **warblers**.

Time and season
Visit in spring for nest-building and courtship displays. All year: **buzzard,** pheasant, stock dove, wood-pigeon, collared dove, tawny owl, green and great spotted woodpeckers, magpie, jay, rook, carrion crow, great, blue, marsh and long-tailed tits, nuthatch, treecreeper, wren, mistle thrush, blackbird, robin, goldcrest, starling, chaffinch. Spring and summer: garden and willow warblers, blackcap, whitethroat, chiffchaff, spotted flycatcher.

HEREFORD AND WORCESTER

36 Clent Hills

LOCATION **South-west of Birmingham, enclosed by the A456, M5 and A491.** *Landranger Sheet 139, 930790.*

These are low, well-drained hills not far from the centre of Birmingham. Fringing the hills are small areas of broad-leaved woodland and a few small ponds; most of the remaining area is covered in grass or gorse bushes. The principal interest is in the breeding population of commoner woodland birds, but in the spring and autumn it may be possible to see a few rarer birds passing – hobby and dotterel have been observed here in the past. The hills are managed as a Country Park, and there are numerous footpaths.

Highlights
Aggressive displays by breeding birds defending their territory.

Time and season
Early spring and summer for breeding birds. All year: **mallard, buzzard, sparrowhawk, kestrel, pheasant,** moorhen, woodcock, stock, turtle and collared doves, wood-pigeon, barn, little and tawny owls, green, great and lesser spotted woodpeckers, carrion crow, rook, jackdaw, magpie, jay, great, blue, coal, marsh and long-tailed tits, nuthatch, treecreeper, wren, goldcrest, mistle thrush, song thrush, blackbird, robin, starling, greenfinch, goldfinch, redpoll, bullfinch, chaffinch. Winter: fieldfare. Spring and summer: turtle dove, swift, swallow, house martin, grasshopper, garden, willow and wood warblers, blackcap, redstart, whitethroat and lesser whitethroat, chiffchaff, pied and spotted flycatchers, tree pipit.

WARWICKSHIRE

37 Charlecote Park

LOCATION **Four miles (7 km) east of Stratford-upon-Avon, north of the B4086.** *Landranger Sheet 151, 263564.*

Charlecote Park was landscaped by 'Capability' Brown; Shakespeare reputedly poached here, and today deer still crop the grass along the banks of the River Avon where it flows through the park. The meandering River Dene is of greater interest to bird-watchers, though, since it has more vegetation at the edges – here you may see kingfisher or **reed bunting.** The other areas of interest are the large trees scattered around the estate, though sadly the huge hollow elms where **kestrel** and **owl** nested were lost to disease.

Highlights
Swallows and **house martins** skimming above the river in summer; large concentrations of **mallard** in winter.

Time and season
Best in summer but good winter population, too; insect-eating birds busiest in the early morning. All year: **heron, mallard, kestrel, pheasant, moorhen, stock dove, wood-pigeon, collared dove, barn owl, magpie, jay, jackdaw, rook, carrion crow, great, blue, coal, marsh,** and **willow tits, nuthatch, treecreeper, wren,** mistle and **song thrushes, blackbird, robin, goldcrest, starling, greenfinch, goldfinch, bullfinch, chaffinch, reed bunting, house sparrow, tree sparrow, green, great** and **lesser spotted woodpeckers.** Winter: **fieldfare, redwing, long-tailed tit.** Spring and summer: **Canada goose, turtle dove, cuckoo, little owl, tawny owl, swift, swallow, house martin, chiffchaff, willow warbler, blackcap, spotted flycatcher, tree pipit.**

NORTHAMPTONSHIRE

38 Salcey Forest

LOCATION **Seven miles (11 km) south of Northampton, on the Buckinghamshire border. Leave Northampton on the A508, and branch off to the left for Wootton** and **Quinton. The forest is 2 miles (3 km) south of Quinton. Park your car in the picnic area.** *Landranger Sheet 152, 792517.*

Before leaving your car, stay there a while and observe the birds which venture forth from the woodland. Regular feeding has made birds such as **greenfinches, nuthatches** and **tits** unusually bold. Salcey Forest is an ancient deciduous woodland, dissected by rides, so although the canopy is dense, most of the woodland birds can be seen from the paths. At the heart of the forest is a large clearing known as Salcey Lawn (formerly used for deer chasing), and its mature oaks provide refuge for **woodpeckers, owls** and **jackdaws.** Make a point of visiting Hartwell Clear Copse – the low, damp undergrowth harbours **nightingales,** and you may hear their song in the late evening, when other birds are more subdued. The busy M1 passes close by to the SE.

Highlights
Nightingale, spotted flycatcher.

Time and season
Summer evenings for **woodcock** and **nightingale,** otherwise early mornings are the most rewarding. All year: **sparrowhawk, kestrel, pheasant, woodcock, stock dove, wood-pigeon, barn owl, little owl, tawny owl, great spotted woodpecker, lesser spotted woodpecker, starling, jay, goldcrest, long-tailed tit, coal tit, nuthatch, chaffinch, greenfinch.** Summer: **turtle dove, nightjar, tree pipit, grasshopper warbler, garden** warbler, blackcap, chiffchaff, spotted flycatcher, nightingale.**

BEDFORDSHIRE

39 The Lodge, Sandy

LOCATION **Two miles (3 km) southeast of Sandy off the B1042. Cross the railway bridge on the outskirts of Sandy and then turn right at a sign for The Lodge about a mile (1.5 km) further on.** *Landranger Sheet 153, 188478.*

Choose one of three waymarked Nature Trails through the Reserve; whichever way you go you will find a wide range of breeding birds in this attractive area of woodland and heath. As the headquarters of the RSPB, you will find all amenities provided for the bird-watcher: hides, picnic area, reception centre and shop. Open from 9 am to 5 pm on weekdays during the summer.

Highlights
Nightjar, redstart, woodcock.

Time and season
April-June is the most rewarding period. All year: **kestrel, woodcock, green woodpecker, great spotted woodpecker, lesser spotted woodpecker, goldcrest, long-tailed tit, coal tit, nuthatch, treecreeper.** Summer: **nightjar, tree pipit, garden warbler, blackcap, willow warbler, chiffchaff, spotted flycatcher, redstart.** Winter: **brambling, siskin, redpoll, crossbill.**

SHROPSHIRE

40 Wenlock Edge

LOCATION Running from Iron-bridge Gorge to Craven Arms. *Landranger Sheet 138, 570965.*

Mixed woodland runs along Wenlock Edge, which is a steep limestone escarpment. The National Trust owns substantial sections of the woods, and from one of them – Easthope Wood – there are good views out towards the Stretton Hills over the countryside around. Bird interest is confined to woodland species; the old trees have many holes suitable for nesting, and the area is popular with birds in passage. Scrubland nearby provides cover and food.

Highlights
Birds of prey soaring over the edge.

Time and season
Small birds in largest numbers in summer. All year: **buzzard, sparrow-hawk, kestrel, woodcock, stock dove, wood-pigeon, tawny owl, great spotted woodpecker, magpie, jay, jackdaw, carrion crow, great, blue, coal, marsh, willow** and **long-tailed tits, treecreeper, wren, mistle** and **song thrushes, blackbird, robin, goldcrest, starling, goldfinch, bullfinch, chaffinch, tree sparrow.** Winter: **little owl, lesser spotted woodpecker, rook, fieldfare, redwing.** Spring and summer: **turtle dove, cuckoo, garden** and **willow** warblers, **blackcap, whitethroat,**

chiffchaff, spotted flycatcher.

41 Dudmaston Estate

LOCATION Four miles (7 km) south-east of Bridgnorth on the A442 to Kidderminster. *Landranger Sheet 138, 746887.*

The large Dudmaston Estate lies in an area of unspoiled countryside in the south of the county. There are 500 acres of woodland, some of it ancient in origin, with a good population of breeding birds. Much of the rest of the Estate is farmland, but the land around the house was landscaped in the 18th C to create a large lake and extensive formal garden. A stretch of the River Severn also borders on the Estate, and wildfowl can be seen both here and on the lake in winter.

Highlights
A large **heronry** with nests occupied most years.

Time and season
Visit in spring to see the **heron** colony at its most active. All year: **mallard, Canada goose, buzzard, sparrow-hawk, kestrel, pheasant, moorhen, woodcock, stock dove, wood-pigeon, turtle dove, collared dove, barn owl, little owl, tawny owl, green, great** and **lesser spotted woodpecker, magpie, jay, jackdaw, rook, carrion crow, great, blue, coal, marsh, willow** and **long-tailed tits, nuthatch, treecreeper, wren, mistle** and **song thrushes, blackbird, robin, goldcrest, grey wagtail, star-**

ling, hawfinch, greenfinch, goldfinch, redpoll, bullfinch, chaffinch, reed bunting, house sparrow, tree sparrow.** Winter: **black-headed gull, fieldfare, redwing, brambling, siskin.** Spring and summer: **heron, cuckoo, swift, swallow, house martin, redstart, nightingale, sedge, garden, willow** and **wood warblers blackcap, whitethroat** and **lesser whitethroat, chiffchaff, spotted flycatcher, tree pipit.**

STAFFORDSHIRE

42 Hawksmoor Nature Reserve

LOCATION One-and-a-half miles (2.5 km) north-east of Cheadle, on the north side of the B5417. *Landranger Sheet 128, 035445.*

The Nature Trail that leads the visitor through this largely wooded Reserve is not planned simply to avoid disturbance to the many nesting birds – among the trees are overgrown mine shafts which pose a genuine hazard. The rich and varied bird population is fairly typical of deciduous woodland, though adjacent pastureland and the river that runs through the area diversifies the range of species that can be seen here. Note – the Nature Trail runs over undulating land, and parts are steep.

Highlights
Most variety in spring and summer. All year: **mallard, sparrowhawk, kestrel, pheasant, moorhen, woodcock, wood-pigeon, tawny owl, green** and **great spotted wood-**

peckers, magpie, jay, jackdaw, rook, carrion crow, great, blue, coal, marsh and long-tailed tits, treecreeper, wren, mistle and song thrushes, blackbird, robin, goldcrest, starling, redpoll, bullfinch, chaffinch, reed bunting, house sparrow, tree sparrow. Winter: fieldfare, redwing. Spring and summer: heron, stock dove, turtle dove, cuckoo, swift, swallow, house martin, redstart, grasshopper, garden, sedge and wood warblers, blackcap, whitethroat and lesser whitethroat, chiffchaff, spotted flycatcher, greenfinch, tree pipit.

CHESHIRE

43 Styal Country Park

LOCATION Half-a-mile (1 km) north-west of Wilmslow. *Landranger Sheet 109, 830830.*

Before walking round the Country Park, pause at the Quarry Bank Mill in Styal. This is the best preserved factory colony of the Industrial Revolution, and is now run as a working museum. Entry to the factory and other buildings costs £2. From the Mill, paths spread through surrounding woods and farmland, with trails running alongside the river. Most of the commoner woodland, water and grassland species can be found at Styal, with tits, finches and warblers particularly numerous in summer. Gulls often use the farmland in winter.

A useful family day out, which ought to entertain even non bird-watchers.

Highlights
A noisy rookery in Altrincham Road.

Time and season
Woodland species most numerous and varied in the summer months. All year: mallard, Canada goose, sparrowhawk, kestrel, pheasant, moorhen, woodcock, black-headed gull, stock dove, wood-pigeon, barn owl, little owl, tawny owl, green, great and lesser spotted woodpecker, magpie, jay, jackdaw, rook, carrion crow, great, blue, coal, marsh, willow and long-tailed tits, treecreeper, wren, mistle and song thrushes, blackbird, robin, goldcrest, grey wagtail, starling, hawfinch, greenfinch, goldfinch, redpoll, bullfinch, chaffinch, reed bunting, tree sparrow. Winter: fieldfare, redwing, siskin, crossbill, brambling. Spring and summer: turtle dove, collared dove, cuckoo, swift, swallow, house martin, redstart, grasshopper, garden, willow and wood warblers, blackcap, whitethroat and lesser whitethroat, chiffchaff, spotted flycatcher, tree pipit.

DERBYSHIRE

44 Dovedale

LOCATION Four to seven miles (6.4-11 km) north-west of Ashbourne. Access by footpath from the A515 Ashbourne to Buxton Road, close to the Alsop-en-le-Dale turn. *Landranger Sheet 119, 153550.* The Trust owns much land in the connecting valleys as well.

The most striking and memorable features of Dovedale are the crags and sheer rock faces, plunging as much as 700 ft (213 m) in places into the deep ravine cut through the limestone by the River Dove. Crag-nesting birds take advantage of the rocks, and other birds forage for food here. The rocks, though, are not the only bird habitat. Much of the valley is wooded, and many small birds breed in the ash and Wych Elm trees. There is scrubland, too; hawthorn and blackthorn bushes provide food for overwintering birds, and shelter for migrants.

Birdlife apart, Dovedale is of course famous as one of the Peak District's most beautiful limestone valleys, and as a major source of inspiration for Isaak Walton's *The Compleat Angler,* in which he describes fishing the River Dove.

Highlights
Loud chorus of birdsong echoing from the vertical valley walls.

Time and season
Visit very early on a spring morning to hear the song birds at their most vocal. All year: mallard, kestrel, pheasant, moorhen, wood-pigeon, tawny owl, green woodpecker, carrion crow, rook, jackdaw, magpie, great, blue, marsh, willow and long-tailed tits, nuthatch, treecreeper, wren, dipper, mistle and song thrushes, blackbird, robin, goldcrest, dunnock, greenfinch, yellowhammer. Spring and summer: wheatear, redstart, blackcap, garden warbler, willow warbler, spotted flycatcher, meadow pipit, grey wagtail, goldfinch, linnet, bullfinch, chaffinch.

NOTTINGHAMSHIRE

45 Clumber Park

LOCATION Two-and-a-half miles (4 km) south-east of Worksop, between the A614 and B6005. *Landranger Sheet 120: entrances at 645774, 626746.*

All that remains of the fine mansion that once stood at the centre of this landscaped park are the chapel and stables. The magnificent grounds, though, give a hint of past splendour, and form a vast and varied haven for the birdlife of the area. There is plenty of woodland – both coniferous and deciduous – farmland, grassland, and a lake. Besides the 75 species of birds that breed here, many wildfowl overwinter on the estate, including whooper and Bewick's swans, and over 1,000 coot.

Highlights
Huge numbers of **finches** roost in Ash Tree Hill Wood.

Time and season
Good throughout the year; stay on until dusk in the summer for **owls, woodcock, nightingale** and **nightjar.** All year: **heron, mallard, Canada goose, sparrowhawk, kestrel, pheasant, moorhen, black-headed gull, stock dove, wood-pigeon, collared dove, tawny owl, green, great** and **lesser spotted woodpecker, jay, jackdaw, rook, carrion crow, great, blue, coal, marsh, willow** and **long-tailed tits, treecreeper, nuthatch, wren, mistle** and **song thrushes, blackbird, robin, goldcrest, starling, hawfinch,** greenfinch, goldfinch, redpoll, bullfinch, chaffinch, house sparrow, tree sparrow. Winter: **Goosander, fieldfare, redwing, firecrest.** Spring and summer: **woodcock, turtle dove, cuckoo, nightjar, woodlark, swift, swallow, house martin, redstart, nightingale, grasshopper, sedge, garden** and **willow warblers, blackcap, whitethroat, chiffchaff, spotted** and **pied flycatchers, tree pipit.**

ESSEX

46 Queen Elizabeth's Hunting Lodge, Epping Forest

LOCATION Epping Forest is a long strip of woodland situated on the north-eastern limits of London. Start your walk from Queen Elizabeth's Lodge near Chingford Green on the A1069, about a mile (1.5 km) south-west of its junction with the A104 (former A11). *Landranger Sheet 177, 398948.*

In spite of its proximity to London, Epping Forest has preserved some 4,000 acres of woodland, albeit crisscrossed with roads and numerous paths. The mature deciduous woodland habitat is likely to hold a fair selection of **treecreepers, tits** and **nuthatches,** although one of the main problems will be actually sighting the birds because of the high level of human disturbance in the area. On Connaught Water, to the north-east of the Lodge, you may see large numbers of **Canada geese, mallard** and **moorhen,** while in the surrounding woods in the winter, small flocks of **finches** may be observed feeding together on the ground. A real test of your observation skills will be to spot the elusive **hawfinch,** before it flies high into the trees.

Highlights
Hawfinch, spotted flycatcher, treecreeper.

Time and season
All year; although you should try to visit as early as possible in the morning when there is least human activity. All year: **Canada goose, mallard, moorhen, green woodpecker, great spotted woodpecker, lesser spotted woodpecker, long-tailed tit, marsh tit, coal tit, black redstart, nuthatch, treecreeper, chaffinch, greenfinch, bullfinch, hawfinch.** Summer: **turtle dove, garden warbler, blackcap, whitethroat, willow warbler, chiffchaff, spotted flycatcher, nightingale.** Winter: **fieldfare, redwing, siskin, redpoll.**

NORFOLK

47 Blickling

LOCATION On the north side of the B1354, 1-2 miles (2 km) north-west of Aylsham on the A140. *Landranger Sheet 133, 178286.*

Most of the 4,700 acre Blickling Estate is farmland, but there are also large areas of woodland, a long stretch of river bank, a lake, and many species-rich hedgerows, all of which provide good and varied habitats for the birds that live here. Some of the woodland areas are of ancient origin and all have interesting birdlife, but Waterloo Wood and Great Wood are the most rewarding. Great Wood is mainly large, well-spaced oaks and Sweet Chestnuts; in Waterloo Wood, there are sycamore trees in addition. The lake and river are worth looking at too, particularly in winter when a variety of wildfowl use them.

Highlights
Lesser spotted woodpecker, and **wood warbler** – scarce in Norfolk.

Time and season
Good at all times, though spring and summer visits will yield more varied sightings. All year: **heron, mallard, sparrowhawk, kestrel, pheasant, moorhen, woodcock, black-headed gull, stock dove, wood-pigeon, collared dove, little owl, tawny owl, green, great** and **lesser spotted woodpecker, magpie, jay, jackdaw, rook, carrion crow, great, blue, coal, marsh, willow** and **long-tailed tits, nuthatch, treecreeper, wren, mistle** and **song thrushes, blackbird, robin, goldcrest, starling, hawfinch, greenfinch, goldfinch, redpoll, bullfinch, chaffinch, reed bunting, house sparrow, tree sparrow.** Winter: **goosander, fieldfare, redwing, grey wagtail, siskin.** Spring and summer: **turtle dove, cuckoo, nightjar, woodlark, swift, swallow, house martin, redstart, nightingale, reed, garden, willow** and **wood warblers, blackcap, whitethroat** and **lesser whitethroat, chiffchaff, spotted flycatcher, tree pipit.**

NORTHERN ENGLAND

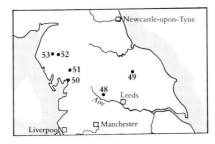

NORTH YORKSHIRE

48 Bolton Abbey Woods

LOCATION Seven miles (11 km) north-west of Ilkley. Take the A65 north-west from Ilkley for 2 miles (3 km), then turn right on to the B6160 for Bolton Abbey. There is a car park on the right about a mile after Bolton Abbey. *Landranger Sheet 104, 075553.*

Lying in the valley of the River Wharfe, Bolton Abbey Woods provide a rich and varied habitat for many woodland and garden birds. On the river banks you may be lucky enough to catch a fleeting glimpse of the kingfisher as it speeds by in a blur of colour; **grey wagtails** and dippers are also known to inhabit the area. Summer visitors include **pied flycatchers** and **redstarts.**

Highlights
Kingfisher, **pied flycatcher.**

Time and season
Spring and early summer are particularly

good. All year: **sparrowhawk, kestrel, woodcock, grey wagtail.**

49 Whitestone Cliff

LOCATION Take the A170 from Thirsk to Scarborough; after 6 miles (10 km) you will arrive at the top of the steep hill known as Sutton Brow. There is a car park on the left, just beyond the turning to Cold Kirby. *Landranger Sheet 100, 515830.*

Some fine trees cling to the escarpment known as Whitestone Cliff, and they provide refuge for an impressive number of woodland birds. As you make your way up to the cliff from the car park, you will pass by some conifer plantations that are favoured by **goldcrest** and **coal tits.** A detour down by Gormire Lake will also reveal not only **moorhens** and **mallard**, but **reed buntings** and **sedge warblers** (summer only) in the reeds at the end of the lake. Where the oaks predominate along the slope, it is possible to see large numbers of **redstarts** in the summer. Splendid views of Gormire Lake are to be had from the top of the escarpment.

Highlights
Redstart, reed bunting, sedge warbler.

Time and season
The dawn chorus is a delight in May and June. All year: **mallard, moorhen, stock dove, wood-pigeon, wren, coal tit, robin, chaffinch, reed bunting.** Summer: **swift, swallow, tree pipit, sedge warbler, garden**

warbler, blackcap, wood warbler, willow warbler, chiffchaff, spotted flycatcher, redstart.

LANCASHIRE

50 Eaves and Waterslack Woods

LOCATION About 2 miles (3 km) south of Arnside. *Landranger Sheet 97, 465758.*

These woods grow on the side of a small hill not far inland from Castlebarrow Head. Oak predominates, but there are substantial areas of ash, beech and hazel, too. The bird population is typical of limestone woodland, with **tits** and **warblers** being the best represented groups. Predators – **owls** and **sparrowhawk** – feed on these smaller birds, and on the voles and mice found on the leafy woodland floor. A Nature Trail starts and finishes at the small car park.

Highlights
Good variety of small birds breeding.

Time and season
Activity throughout the year, but most interesting in the spring. All year: **sparrowhawk, pheasant, woodcock, wood-pigeon, tawny owl, green** and **great spotted woodpeckers, carrion crow, magpie, jay, great, blue, marsh** and **long-tailed tits, treecreeper, wren, song thrush, blackbird, robin, bullfinch, chaffinch.** Spring and summer: **willow warbler, chiffchaff, wood warbler, spotted flycatcher.**

CUMBRIA

51 Sizergh Castle

LOCATION Three-and-a-half miles (5.5 km) south of Kendal, to the west of the A6. *Landranger Sheet 97, 498878.*

Sizergh Castle and ornamental garden are open to the public only on a limited basis during the summer (there is an entrance fee payable) but there is unlimited free access to the surrounding grounds throughout the year. Birdlife here is rich and varied, largely because the estate straddles several different habitat types; although lowland grassland and woods predominate, there are riverside communities where the River Kent flows along the extreme eastern edge of the estate. There are also scattered trees and scrub on the open grassland, providing protection for nesting and roosting birds.

Highlights
Birds of prey can often be seen hovering over the area.

Time and season
Something happening all year round – passing migrants add more species to this list during autumn and spring. All year: **heron, mallard, goosander, buzzard, sparrowhawk, kestrel, pheasant, moorhen, wood-pigeon, collared dove, barn, tawny** and **little owls, green woodpecker, carrion crow, rook, magpie, jay, great, blue, willow** and **long-tailed tits, treecreeper, wren, song thrush,**

---

robin, redstart, hawfinch. Winter: **waxwing, fieldfare, siskin, brambling.** Spring and summer: **curlew, cuckoo, swift, swallow, blackcap, whitethroat, lesser whitethroat, willow warbler, chiffchaff, spotted flycatcher, dunnock, tree pipit, grey wagtail.**

---

52 Ullswater: Glencoyne Park and Woods

LOCATION On the western shore of Ullswater at the southern end. *Landranger Sheet 90, 390195 and 385180; Outdoor Leisure Map: The English Lakes NE.*

For birds, the importance of these lake-edge woodland properties lies in their diversity: not just in terms of the variety of tree species, but also in their ages. Besides new growth, there is an abundance of large trees – mature oak, holly, and ash – and plenty of dead wood on the ground. Both the woods and the park overlook Ullswater, so it is possible to see water-birds here as well as woodland species and the proximity of crags and moorland means that upland birds can often be observed soaring overhead. The nearby Aira Force waterfall is also worth a visit in the spring – dipper and common sandpiper breed there.

Highlights
Variety and abundance of breeding birds.

Time and season
For woodland species, spring and summer is the best time to visit; the

water and upland add interest at other times. All year: **heron, mallard, red-breasted merganser, goosander, buzzard, sparrowhawk, kestrel, moorhen, woodcock, stock dove, wood-pigeon, barn owl, tawny owl, great spotted woodpecker, magpie, jay, jackdaw, rook, carrion crow, great, blue, coal, marsh** and **long-tailed tits, treecreeper, wren, mistle** and **song thrushes, blackbird, robin, goldcrest, grey wagtail, greenfinch, chaffinch, reed bunting, tree sparrow.** Spring and summer: **swift, green woodpecker, swallow, house martin, redstart, sedge warbler, blackcap, garden warbler, whitethroat, willow warbler, chiffchaff, wood warbler, pied** and **spotted flycatchers, tree pipit.**

53 Great Wood, Keswick

LOCATION **One mile (1.5 km) south of Keswick, along the east side of the Borrowdale road.** *Landranger Sheet 89, 275215; Outdoor Leisure Map: The English Lakes NW.*

This lakeside wood stretches from flat land near Derwentwater up to steep crags in the east, and is mainly coniferous. However, there is broadleaved woodland on the steep crags, and by the water, and it is in these areas that the greatest variety of birds is to be found. The commoner oakwood species dominate, and the large lake contributes a wildfowl community that makes this an interesting site to visit even during the winter months. Keep an eye open for mammals, too.

Highlights
Nuthatch, which rarely breed this far north, can be seen in the woods.

Time and season
Interesting most times of year. All year: **heron, mallard, red-breasted merganser, sparrowhawk, kestrel, pheasant, moorhen, woodcock, stock dove, wood-pigeon, tawny owl, green, great** and **lesser spotted woodpeckers, magpie, jay, jackdaw, rook, carrion crow, great, blue, coal,** and **long-tailed tits, nuthatch, treecreeper, wren, mistle** and **song thrushes, blackbird, robin, goldcrest, goldfinch, bullfinch, chaffinch, house sparrow, tree sparrow.** Winter: **black-headed gull, fieldfare, redwing.** Spring and summer: **cuckoo, swift, swallow, redstart, garden, willow** and **wood warblers, blackcap, chiffchaff, pied flycatcher, tree pipit.**

SCOTLAND

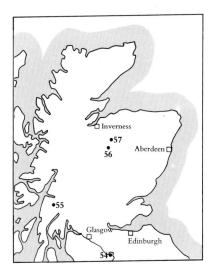

STRATHCLYDE

54 Falls of Clyde

LOCATION **One mile (1.5 km) south of Lanark. Leave Lanark on the A73, but after quarter-of-a-mile (0.5 km) turn right and follow signs for New Lanark. The Falls of Clyde are immediately south of New Lanark.** *Landranger Sheet 71, 882425.*

Here the River Clyde tumbles its way through a deep wooded gorge, leaving a series of waterfalls in its wake. Most of the surrounding land is managed by the Scottish Wildlife Trust, and you will find riverside walks clearly marked. A substantial population of **warblers** inhabit the woods in the summer season, while in the winter the valley provides winter quarters for **fieldfares, redwings** and **bramblings**.

Highlights
Pied flycatcher, grey wagtail.

Times and season
All year; look out for **redstarts** in the summer and **redwings** in the winter. All year: **stock dove, green woodpecker, great spotted woodpecker, grey wagtail, goldcrest, long-tailed tit, willow tit, coal tit, treecreeper, siskin, redpoll.** Summer: **turtle dove, garden warbler, blackcap, willow warbler, chiffchaff, pied flycatcher, redstart.**

55 Inverliever Forest

LOCATION **Take the A85 east from Oban to Taynuilt, then turn right towards Kilchrenan on the B845. After Kilchrenan turn right on to an unclassified road towards Ford.** *Landranger Sheet 55, 998178.*

Overlooking Loch Awe, this splendid forest of largely mature conifers holds a variety of woodland birds, notably **siskins** and **tree pipits.** Occasionally you may see a **crested tit** creeping carefully along the trunks of pine trees, searching the bark for insects. In the autumn the loch receives a number of winter visitors, including the whooper swan. Details of forest walks can be obtained from the Forest Office, Dalavich.

Highlights
Crested tit, siskin.

Time and season
All year: **buzzard, kestrel, woodcock, great spotted woodpecker, crested tit, siskin.** Summer: **tree pipit, pied flycatcher, redstart.**

HIGHLAND

56 Glen More

LOCATION **From Aviemore take the unclassified road to Cairn Gorm. Stop at the Glen More Camp Site opposite the Information Centre.** *Landranger Sheet 36, 978098.*

Glen More must rank among the finest bird haunts in Britain. It combines a mixture of habitats: mature Scots Pine forest, dense scrubby woodland and thickly planted conifer stands. A number of streams run through the glen, feeding Loch Morlich below and providing ideal conditions for dippers and **grey wagtails.** Also look out for Scottish **crossbills.**

Highlights
Crested tit, Scottish crossbill.

Time and season
An early morning walk in April, May or June may reveal not only the best variety of resident and breeding birds, but also capercaillie and roe deer. All year: **buzzard, sparrowhawk, woodcock, wood-pigeon, tawny owl, great spotted woodpecker,** skylark, meadow pipit, **mistle thrush, grey wagtail, wren, goldcrest, crested tit, coal tit, robin, mistle thrush, chaf-**finch, siskin, redpoll, crossbill. Summer: **cuckoo, swift, willow warbler, spotted flycatcher, redstart.**

57 Loch Garten

LOCATION **Take the A95 north from Aviemore towards Grantown-on-Spey. One mile (1.5 km) past Kinveachy, follow signs to the right for Boat of Garten. Loch Garten can be reached from a minor road off the B970.** *Landranger Sheet 36, 981183.*

The Abernethy Forest, on the shores of Loch Garten, is an ancient and well-established tract of Scots Pine woodland, and consequently supports a rich variety of breeding birds. Old Scots Pines, interspersed with birch trees and juniper bushes, provide a fine habitat for numerous small passerines, including **crested tits, crossbills** and **siskins,** while dense young plantations hold large numbers of **willow warblers, robins** and **goldcrests.** Loch Garten has the added bonus of its osprey eyrie.

Highlights
Crested tit, Scottish crossbill.

Time and season
All year: **sparrowhawk, woodcock, wood-pigeon, tawny owl, great spotted woodpecker, grey wagtail, wren, goldcrest, long-tailed tit, crested tit, coal tit, great tit, robin, mistle thrush, treecreeper, chaf-finch, siskin, crossbill.** Summer: **tree pipit, willow warbler, spotted flycatcher, redstart.**

Understanding birds

It is a bird's feathers that make it unique. There are other animals which fly, sing, make nests, lay eggs or migrate. But only birds have feathers. The nearest any other creature comes to having feathers is the reptile with its scales. Feathers probably evolved from scales, and birds and reptiles such as crocodiles and dinosaurs, for all their immense differences, shared a common ancestor.

Scientists are unable to tell exactly how the change from scales to feathers took place. Fossils of *Archaeopteryx,* the first known bird, show that 150 million years ago feathers were already the same as they are today. But *Archaeopteryx* was no ordinary bird. Although it had feathers, it still had the teeth and long, bony tail of a reptile. Its breastbone was poorly developed and lacked the deep keel to which the flight muscles of modern birds are anchored. This suggests that at best it could only flap its wings weakly. Probably it relied mostly on gliding.

Their mastery of the air is the main reason why birds have been one of nature's most spectacular successes, evolving into thousands of different species and colonising every corner of the globe. In every aspect of their physiology, they reveal how perfectly they are adapted for flight. Some bones which were separate in their flightless ancestors – including bones in the wings and sections of the backbone – are now fused together, giving greater strength. Others are hollow and strutted, combining strength with lightness. Massive breast muscles power their wings, while their hearts keep pace with their intense energy, beating with fantastic rapidity; in the case of a robin's heart, for instance, more than eight times as fast as a man's. Birds' eyesight is also the most acute in the animal world, adapted to gathering information at the same high speed at which they live.

Speed, infinite mobility and wildness: these are the characteristics common to all birdlife, which make birds so fascinating to watch. Birds rarely remain still, except when they are roosting or incubating their eggs, and they are always on the alert. But their actions are never without meaning; every movement a bird makes has an exact purpose. One of the greatest satisfactions in bird-watching is understanding why birds behave as they do – learning to tell the difference between threat and courtship displays, for instance, or observing how they look after their feathers or build their nests.

Bird classification
It is now established that there are some 8,600 different kinds of birds in the world. At one time the number was put as high as 25,000, partly because the same bird had different names in different parts of the world. This was before the modern system of classification had been developed, which groups birds according to their evolutionary relationship with one another, and gives each of them a set of scientific names.

The basic unit of the modern system is the species, an interbreeding group of identical birds. The next, larger division is the genus, a group of closely related species of birds, usually showing obvious similarities. The black-headed gull, for instance, is one of many species belonging to the gull genus. A bird's scientific name always states the genus first, then the species. The black-headed gull is called *Larus ridibundus* – translated literally, the name means 'Gull, laughing'.

When one genus closely resembles another, they are grouped together to make a family. Gulls are similar in many ways to terns, and both belong to the family *Laridae,* named after the Greek word for a gull; in some schemes of classification they are separated into sub-families, *Larinae* (gulls) and *Sterninae* (terns). The families are grouped into 27 different orders. The family of gulls and terns belongs, together with a great variety of other sea- and shore-birds, in the order *Charadriiformes,* after the Greek for 'plover'. All the orders together make up the zoological class *Aves* – 'Birds'.

Keeping records
To become a really proficient bird-watcher, it is important to keep a field notebook, such as this one, and to keep a logbook at home in which to write up your notes in greater detail. Your notebooks will soon become an invaluable memory bank, fund of knowledge and aid for identification at subsequent sightings.

At the end of each year, check through your notes to see if they are worth sending to the records committee of your local bird-watching society. The annual bird reports of these societies, combined on a national level, often form the basis on which professional ornithologists establish the current status of a species.

Taking part in a census

Once you have become experienced at bird-watching you may wish to take part in a detailed census, organised at a local or national level. A census can take the form of a monthly count of birds at a reservoir or estuary, to check on the numbers of wildfowl or waders, for instance; or in the spring and summer months it may entail finding out the breeding population of a particular area. One such census is the Nest Record Scheme, co-ordinated by the British Trust for Ornithology, which aims to establish the exact breeding status of all British birds. If you wish to join this scheme, contact the BTO at Beech Grove, Tring, Hertfordshire.

Alternatively, you may prefer to start your own project. This could take the form of a census of the birds seen in your garden at different times of the year, or you could study the change in the type and number of birds on land undergoing development. Bird populations are always fluctuating, and keeping track of the changes taking place around you can be a fascinating pastime.

Bird ringing

The method of catching birds and ringing them – putting a light metal band on one leg – has been in use since the end of the 19th century, as a way of studying bird behaviour and migrations and to help in the conservation of particular species. Ringing birds has enabled conservationists to find out where certain species stop to rest while on migration; and international agreements between governments have made some of these stop-over points into nature reserves, to help to ensure the survival of the species.

The most common way of trapping birds in order to ring them is by using mist-nets – black nylon or terylene nets which are almost invisible to a bird in flight. The ringer quickly and carefully removes the trapped bird from the net, then fits the ring on its leg. The ring carries the address of the BTO, and a number which is unique to that bird. Before being released, the bird is identified and weighed and full details are taken of its age, sex and condition. The records are then sent for processing and storage to the BTO. If you wish to become a ringer yourself, you must be trained by a recognised expert and obtain a permit from the BTO. As co-ordinators of the ringing scheme in this country, the BTO will supply any information which you may require.

If you ever find a dead, ringed bird, remove the ring and send it to the BTO, with details about when and where you found the bird and, if you can tell, what may have caused its death. They will then send you all the information gathered about the bird when it was originally ringed. Never attempt to remove a ring from the leg of a living bird, as birds' bones are very fragile and can easily be broken.

Photographing birds

Bird photography requires great patience, as well as expensive equipment and considerable technical skill; but, if you can afford it, it is one of the most satisfying activities which an amateur bird-watcher can perform.

The most suitable camera is a single-lens reflex camera, with interchangeable lenses and a through-the-lens metering system. At least one telephoto lens of not less than 200 mm focal length is essential; this will enable you to photograph birds in close-up without alarming them. A tripod and cable release will help to eliminate blurred pictures caused by camera shake.

Remember how easily birds can be disturbed, and never do anything which threatens their welfare. Disturbing birds in the breeding season often causes them to desert their eggs or young, and for certain species the law requires that you have a licence before photographing them at the nest. The Royal Society for the Protection of Birds publishes a booklet, *Wild Birds and the Law,* which lists all the protected species.

Many species of birds are heard more often than they are seen, and in recent years recording bird-song has become an increasingly popular hobby among bird-watchers. As with photography, it is necessary to choose your equipment with great care, and preferably with expert guidance; but even with inexpensive tape-recorders it is possible to achieve many interesting results.

Societies and journals

The best way to make contact with other bird-watchers is to join your local bird-watching society. These societies often organise weekend excursions to nature reserves and sanctuaries, and also have occasional films and lectures presented by experts. These meetings are excellent opportunities to discuss any problems you may have with bird identification or understanding individual bird behaviour, as well as for gaining advice on the purchase of equipment. The annual bird reports which they publish will give you much useful information about the birds in your own area. Most public libraries can tell you the addresses of local societies, and how to join them.

There are also several national ornithological societies, some of which you may wish to join. The major societies are listed below, together with a selection of their journals about bird-watching.

BRITISH ORNITHOLOGISTS' UNION *c/o The Zoological Society of London, Regent's Park, London NW1 4RY.* One of the world's foremost ornithological societies, chiefly for professional ornithologists, or advanced amateurs. It holds occasional meetings, with lectures or films on any aspect of world ornithology. Publishes *Ibis,* a quarterly journal which contains articles covering a wide range of subjects related to birds.

BRITISH TRUST FOR ORNITHOLOGY *Beech Grove, Station Road, Tring, Hertfordshire.* Similar to the BOU, but deals solely with British birds. Runs the national ringing scheme, the Common Birds Census, and various other educational or research projects. Publishes the journal *Bird Study.*

IRISH WILDBIRD CONSERVANCY *Southview, Church Road, Greystones, Co Wicklow, Ireland.* The Irish equivalent of the BTO.

ROYAL SOCIETY FOR THE PROTECTION OF BIRDS *The Lodge, Sandy, Bedfordshire.* Owns and manages some of the most important nature reserves in Britain. Runs courses for beginners in many parts of the country, and publishes *Birds,* a quarterly magazine dealing with all aspects of bird-watching.

SCOTTISH ORNITHOLOGISTS CLUB *21 Regent Terrace, Edinburgh, Scotland.* Similar aims to the BTO, with particular reference to bird-watching and birdlife in Scotland.

THE WILDFOWL TRUST *Slimbridge, Gloucestershire.* Mainly concerned with the conservation of wildfowl. Manages several important sanctuaries where wild ducks, geese and swans can be observed at close quarters. Publishes *Wildfowl,* an annual report containing articles about wildfowl, and information about the Trust's collection.

ROYAL SOCIETY FOR NATURE CONSERVATION *The Green, Nettleham, Lincoln LN2 2NR.* Parent body of the Nature Conservation Trusts, which manages more than 1,300 reserves, many of which provide facilities.

The bird-watcher's code

Whatever you choose to do as a bird-watcher – whether you prefer travelling widely to watch birds, or setting up a hide in one place, whether you are photographing, recording or counting birds – there is a code of conduct always to be observed.

Never cause undue disturbance to birds, especially in the breeding season.
Always obtain permission before venturing on to private land.
Keep to paths as far as possible.
Never park so as to block the entrance to a field.
Leave gates as you find them.
Leave no litter.
When you have finished watching a bird, leave quietly in order not to frighten it.

Glossary

A

Accidental Uncommon visitor, arriving only when blown off course or disorientated; same as VAGRANT.

Adult Bird with fully developed final plumage.

Albino Bird with partial or total absence of dark pigment, giving it a white appearance. In a true albino, dark pigment is completely absent from the beak, eyes and legs, as well as from the plumage.

Axillaries Feathers in the axilla, or 'armpit'.

B

Barb Branch of the central shaft of a feather.

Barbule Branch of the BARB of a feather.

Bastard wing Group of feathers at first digit of wing from tip, or 'thumb'.

Blaze Coloured patch at base of bill.

Breeding plumage Plumage developed during the breeding season.

Brood patch Area of featherless, thickened skin on abdomen developed as an aid to incubating eggs.

C

Call Brief sound used for contact within a species, to warn of danger, and so on. Same throughout the year.

Carpal joint Forward-pointing joint of the wing when closed: the 'wrist'.

Cere Fleshy covering at base of bill found in hawks, pigeons and other birds. Often distinctively coloured.

Colony Gathering of some species of birds, to breed or roost.

Contour feathers Feathers lying along the body, streamlining it and insulating it against cold.

Coverts Feathers overlying the bases of the tail feathers or major wing feathers; for example tail covert, wing covert, under-wing covert. Also the area of feathers covering a bird's ear (also known as the ear covert).

Crepuscular Active only at dusk and dawn.

D

Dialect Local variation in the song of a bird population.

Display Posturing, usually by male bird to attract female during breeding season; also to warn off rival males, and to defend TERRITORY.

Diurnal Active only in daylight hours.

Dorsal Belonging to a bird's back.

Down First feather covering of young birds of some species.

E

Eclipse Post-breeding moult, characteristic of ducks, during which for a short time, males become flightless, lose their bright plumage and come to resemble females.

Egg-tooth Horny protuberance at tip of upper MANDIBLE of a chick, used to crack shell when emerging.

Eruption Mass movement of birds, occurring at irregular intervals.

Escape Species or individual bird escaped or liberated from captivity.

Exotic Term describing a species foreign to an area.

Eye-stripe Distinctively coloured stripe of feathers leading back from or through the eye.

F

Feral Term describing wild bird population that originated in captivity.

First year Period between the time a bird leaves the nest and the following breeding season.

Fore-edge, fore-wing Leading edge of wing.

G

Gape Angle of bill opening.

H

Hawking Capture of flying insects while bird is on the wing.

Hood Area of contrasting plumage covering most of head.

I

Immature Bird in plumage indicating lack of sexual maturity.

Introduced Term describing birds captured in one area and released in another.

Invasion Sudden mass arrival of birds not usually seen in an area.

J

Juvenile Bird in its first covering of true feathers.

L

Lek Place where males of some species, for example black grouse, display communally prior to breeding.

Lore Area between base of upper mandible and eye.

M

Mandible Upper or lower part of bill.

Mantle Back.

Melanistic Term describing a bird with an abnormally large amount of dark pigment in its plumage.

Migrant Species that does not remain on its breeding grounds all year.

Mob Aggression, usually directed by a number of birds against a predator.

Morph Same as PHASE.

Moustachial stripe Streak of contrasting feathers running back from the base of the bill.

N

Nail Shield or horny plate at tip of upper mandible, found in some geese and ducks.

Nidiculous Term describing young that are hatched helpless and blind, and stay in nest for a considerable time.

Nidifugous Term describing young that are hatched with eyes open, covered with down and able to leave nest almost immediately.

Nocturnal Active only during darkness – typically in relation to owls.

O

Oceanic Another word for PELAGIC.

Orbital ring Fleshy ring around the eye.

P

Partial migrant Species of which some individuals migrate, but others remain on their breeding grounds.

Passage migrant Bird usually breeding and wintering outside an area, but regularly seen on migration.

Pelagic Term describing sea-bird that seldom or never visits land except in breeding season.

Phase Distinctive variation of plumage within a species.

Preen gland Gland on rump that exudes oil as an aid to preening.

Primary feathers A bird's main flight feathers, attached to 'hand'.

R

Race Term used to describe a subspecies of a bird which inhabits a different region and has slightly different physical characteristics, as for example, plumage pattern.

Raptor Bird of prey, excluding owls.

Resident Bird present throughout year – as opposed to a migrant.

S

Scapulars Feathers above the shoulders of a bird.

Secondary feathers Flight feathers attached to 'forearm'.

Sedentary Term describing species that does not migrate or move far from its breeding ground.

Song Language of a bird, intended to identify its TERRITORY to other birds and attract females to intended breeding area.

Speculum Contrasting patch of SECONDARY FEATHERS in wing, usually in ducks.

Spinning Action of some water birds, for example phalaropes, swimming in tight circles to bring food to the surface.

Stoop Term describing dive of a raptor, especially peregrine falcon.

Sub-song Subdued song outside period of full song, or by young males.

Subspecies See RACE.

Superciliary stripe Streak of contrasting feathers above a bird's eye.

T

Tarsus Part of a bird's leg from directly above the toes to the first joint.

Territory Part of a habitat defended by the bird or group of birds occupying it against other birds.

V

Vagrant Uncommon visitor, arriving only when blown off course or disorientated.

Ventral Belonging to a bird's underside or belly.

W

Wattles Fleshy protuberances on head.

Web Flesh between toes of water birds.

Wing-bar Conspicuous stripe across the wing, formed by tips of feathers of contrasting colour.

Wing linings Under-wing COVERTS.

Winter plumage Plumage developed outside breeding season, by male or female bird.

Winter visitor Bird that usually breeds outside the area in which it is seen in winter.

Index

BIRDS

B
blackbird 69
blackcap 55
brambling 85
bullfinch 91
bunting, cirl 95
 reed 94
buzzard 19

C
chaffinch 86
chiffchaff 61
crossbill 92
 two-barred 92
crow, carrion 48
 hooded 48
cuckoo 29

D
dove, collared 28
 rock 26
 stock 26
 turtle 27
dunnock 51

F
fieldfare 72
firecrest 62
flycatcher, pied 64
 spotted 63

G
goldcrest 60
goldfinch 90
goosander 17
goose, Canada 15
grebe, great crested 12
greenfinch 88
gull, black-headed 24

H
hawfinch 93
heron 13

J
jackdaw 46

jay 45

K
kestrel 20

M
magpie 44
mallard 14
martin, house 39
merganser, red-breasted 16
moorhen 22

N
nightingale 67
nightjar 34
nutcracker 45
nuthatch 81

O
owl, barn 30
 little 32
 tawny 31

P
pheasant 21
 red-throated 42
pipit, tree 42

R
redpoll 89
redstart 65
 black 66
redwing 73
robin 68
rook 47

S
siskin 87
sparrow, house 84
 tree 83
sparrowhawk 18
starling 43
swallow 38
swift 33

T
thrush, mistle 71
 song 70
tit, blue 78
 coal 79
 crested 76
 great 80
 long-tailed 75
 marsh 74
 willow 77
treecreeper 82

W
wagtail, grey 41
warbler, garden 54
 grasshopper 52
 sedge 53
 willow 58
 wood 59
waxwing 49
whitethroat 56
 lesser 57
woodcock 23
woodlark 40
woodpecker, great spotted 36
 green 35
 lesser spotted 37
wood-pigeon 25
wren 50

SITES

A
Alice Holt Forest 106-7

B
Barle Valley 102
Blickling 116-17
Bolton Abbey Woods 117
Boscastle Harbour 99-100
Box Hill 107-8

C
Castle Drogo 101
Castle Woods 110
Charlecote Park 112-13
Chart, The 108
Cheddar Cliffs 102-3
Clent Hills 112
Clumber Park 116
Colby Estate 109-10
Cotehele 99
Craigllech Woods 111

D
Dinas Hill 110
Dovedale 115
Dudmaston Estate 114
Durford Heath 105

E
Eaves Woods 118
Epping Forest 116
Erdigg 111

F
Falls of Clyde 119-20
Fowey 98

G
Glencoyne Park and Woods
    118-19
Glen More 120
Great Wood, Keswick 119

H
Hawksmoor Nature Reserve
    114-15
Helford River 98
Henrhyd Falls 111
Hindhead 107
Holmwood Common 107

I
Inverliever Forest 120

K
Killerton 101-2

L
Lanhydrock 98-9
Limpsfield Common 108
Loch Garten 120
Lynmouth 100-1

M
Milford, Little 110
Mottisfont Abbey, 103-4

N
Nap Wood 106
Newark Park 112
Nymans Gardens 105-6

P
Parke 101
Plym Bridge Woods 100
Portland Bill 103

Q
Queen Elizabeth Country Park
    104
Queen Elizabeth's Hunting
    Lodge 116

S
Salcey Forest 113
Sandy, The Lodge 113-14
Selborne Hill 104
Sizergh Castle 118

Stourhead 106
Styal Country Park 115
Sugar Loaf 109

V
Valencey Valley 99-100
Virginia Water 108-9

W
Wakehurst Place 105
Waterslack Woods 118
Wenlock Edge 114
Whitestone Cliff 117-18

Acknowledgements

The editor and publishers would like to thank the following for their invaluable help in compiling information for this book:

Katherine Hearn (Assistant Adviser on Conservation) and Keith Alexander (Surveyor, Biological Survey Team), National Trust.

The Sussex Trust for Nature Conservation.

Editorial and design
Researched, written and edited by Michele Staple and Richard Platt; assistant editor Rosemary Dawe; designed by Arthur Brown; map on page 96 by Line and Line.

GARDEN & WOODLAND BIRDS
is based on the Reader's Digest Field Guide to Birds of Britain to which the following made major contributions:

CONSULTANTS AND AUTHORS
Dr Philip J.K. Burton, British Museum (Natural History)
Robert Gillmor   Howard Ginn, M.A.
Wildlife Advisory Branch, Nature Conservancy Council
T.W. Parmenter
John Parslow, Director (Conservation),
Royal Society for the Protection of Birds
Cyril A. Walker, British Museum (Natural History)
D.I.M. Wallace, B.A.

ARTISTS

Stephen Adams	Hermann Heinzel
Norman Arlott	Mick Loates
Peter Barrett	Sean Milne
Trevor Boyer	Robert Morton
John Busby	D.W. Ovenden
John Francis	Patrick Oxenham
Robert Gillmor	Jim Russell
Tim Hayward	Ken Wood

CARTOGRAPHY
The distribution maps were based on information supplied by John Parslow and prepared by Clyde Surveys Ltd